I0149269

Not Ashamed of the Gospel

Confessions of a Liberal Charismatic

by

Henry E. Neufeld

Energion Publications
P. O. Box 841
Gonzalez, FL 32560
http://www.energionpubs.com
pubs@energion.com

Energion Publications
P. O. Box 841
Gonzalez, FL 32560

Cover design by Carol Everhart Roper,
PhotoMD (www.photomd.net)

ISBN: 1-893729-37-0

Preface

I'm certain this little book is going to bring on at least two questions: First, what is a liberal charismatic and second, how can one be both liberal and charismatic?

The answer is that I'm not sure what a liberal charismatic is, and I'm not sure that I'm liberal, though the title doesn't scare me as it does some people. The title "liberal charismatic" was given to me by an opponent in online discussion. I've mentioned it to audiences several times since when I have spoken, and some of them say there may be a point to it. In addition, I use it precisely because people will ask questions. Some will even be turned off about this book before they open the cover because of the dreaded 'L' word.

So why do some people say it is appropriate as a label for me, and why do I embrace (or at least "sort of" embrace) this title that was given to me as an accusation?

First, it is somewhat appropriate. I believe in a Christian faith that is to a large extent driven by experience, and that is not limited very much by doctrines. It is defined at its center by the command of Jesus to love God will all my heart and my neighbor as myself. To those who would say Christianity is really defined by the incarnation I would say that the incarnation embodies those two principles in a way that nothing else could. I make it a principle both of life and of Biblical interpretation to try to hang everything off of those commands, just as Jesus said that the whole law and the prophets could be hung there. Because of this, I embrace many people who would seem doctrinally incompatible as brothers and sisters in the faith. I welcome dialogue, friendship, and cooperation with people who share with me only the love of one's fellow human beings. This could be regarded as liberal. But you'll find while reading these pages that I also hold some doctrinal positions that are not generally regarded as liberal, and some that are regarded as very conservative.

Second, I believe in Christian unity. By this I do not mean the unification of Christianity under one banner that I select. I don't ask to define what "true" Christianity is. You get to define that, hopefully in your own dialogue with God. I mean working in unity in whatever we can agree on, and not judging one another, and not setting our own agendas for other people.

Christian unity in this sense does not mean an end of denominations and congregations, but it does mean an end to the stranglehold of organizations on Christian faith and Christian fellowship. I call on the individual to walk with God and to find a community with which they can walk with God, no matter how that community is defined. Find the fellowship with which you can work and serve.

Right now there are movements trying to unite charismatic and evangelical believers, and many movements for uniting groups of mainline and liberal believers, but there is a barrier between the evangelicals and charismatics on the one hand and liberal Christians on the other. I think I scare people on both sides of the line when I embrace believers from all of these streams, including the many variations within them. From revivalist to traditionalist, from liberal to fundamentalist, from charismatic to cessationist, we all have something to learn from one another, and we all have something to teach.

Unfortunately, we very often cut ourselves off from communication with one stream or another simply because we assume they are past the limits. There are some who cut *themselves* off from communication. I find myself hard pressed to find a reason to talk to and listen to some groups. But if we can listen to the broadest possible range of people, and let others be the ones who cut ties and build walls, I believe that would show the practice of God's love within the Christian community.

But let me go one step further. Let's not unite as Christians in order to combat all those of other religions or people of no religion. Let's unite as a witness. Let's unite to show what God's love can do when it is displayed through a group of people who care more about loving one another than they do about whether their theology is in perfect order, or whether their beliefs are perfectly correct, or whether they are socially acceptable to us. Let's not be embarrassed over who we associate with any more than Jesus was.

There are some who will ask whether this book is intended as evangelistic. In one sense, I will say yes. I have gained great peace through my relationship to God through Jesus Christ, and I value my experiences. I'm sharing that in this book. If you don't want to read what I have to share, don't read the book. I say that seriously and without offense. You can tell me directly that you're not interested if you like. It's not a problem. I firmly believe your relationship to God, if any, is strictly your business and God's.

But there is another sense of evangelism, which is commonly called proselytizing. I'm not doing that. You will find here no impassioned plea from me asking you to accept Jesus Christ as your savior. I am telling you that I have done so. I'm sharing my experiences and my understanding of those experiences. I'd like you to come alongside and try to understand me and dialogue with me through the words of this book.

But I view this sharing much as I view the way God shared with humanity through Jesus. He is infinite, or something so close to that we can't tell the difference, and we are finite. In Jesus God crossed that gap—by definition as wide a gap as is possible—and asked us to share with him. I'm speaking across a much narrower gap, infinitely narrower, and I'm asking you to share with me.

God is not the God of the gaps—the one who fills in the spaces where we don't understand. He is the God who crosses gaps, and invites us to cross them with him and for him.

Everything is from God, who was reconciling the world to himself through Christ, and who has given us the task of reconciliation. – 2 Corinthians 5:18

Following my personal testimony, which is the first chapter, I have used Romans 1:16-17 as an outline for this book. Please be aware that I am not providing an exegesis of that passage, nor am I claiming that this is a work of Pauline theology. This book relates my personal experiences, and my understanding, based on many scriptures and many sources. But I found that the key elements of that passage provide me with the right titles, and I'm using the passage to organize the very diverse material.

I am not ashamed of the good news, for it is God's power for salvation to everyone who believes, to the Jew first, and also to the Greek. For in the good news it was shown that God was right, going from faith to faith, as it has been written, "The one who is righteous will live by faith." – Romans 1:16-17

Table of Contents

A Personal Testimony

I intended to add this chapter as an appendix, but I feel led to include it first. This section describes my personal experience with God. The following chapters, following the outline I got from the wording of Romans 1:16-17, provide a personalized theology that I have built from my study and experience. The two go together. If you don't want to read the story, you can go to the next chapter. But in my understanding of theology, the story is the key. That's why I believe this story needs to come first.

As you read it here, this testimony includes the bulk of the material from the testimony as posted on my web site, (http://energion.com/rpp/drawn.shtml), and included as an appendix to my study guide on the book of Hebrews (*To the Hebrews: A Participatory Study Guide*, ISBN: 1-893729-23-0), where it formed a substantial part of my explanation for my understanding of Hebrews 6, falling away, and grieving the Holy Spirit.

In my understanding of theology, the story is the key.

I grew up as the son of Seventh-day Adventist missionary parents. I don't intend to tell the entire story of my life, but I want to lay a foundation for what happens later. My parents have great faith, and they demonstrated that faith in their daily lives and in the way they conducted mission work. My father was a medical doctor and my mother a registered nurse. My father prayed with every patient he treated.

Some missionaries felt it was alright to smuggle things through borders in order to carry out their work (and in some cases I believe they are right), but my parents did not work that way. They would load medical supplies for which they had no import license right in the open. Before approaching the border control point we would stop and pray, and then proceed through. Inevitably the inspector would notice the material we were carrying and would ask what it was. My father would always say, "Medical supplies" or whatever it was we were transporting for our work. The inspector would then ask for the import license, and my father would indicate he didn't have one. Every time this happened we were simply waved on through the border. We were never detained nor were any of the supplies confiscated.

I was enrolled in the pre-Law program of the college, and had collected all the computer cards for the classes in that program. I went back, cancelled them all, and started the Biblical languages program.

In 1971 we traveled to Guyana, South America, where my father underwent emergency surgery soon after our arrival. We were told that he was unlikely to work again or to live more than 25 years. My parents called for the elders of the church, as indicated in James 5, who anointed him and prayed for his healing. Within two weeks he had taken over as the sole physician for a 54 bed hospital. (This story is available in the booklet *Directed Paths*, ISBN: 1-893729-22-2, available from Energion Publications.)

I was very firm about my faith and about its Biblical base. I felt the call of God to teaching ministry during registration for my second year of college. This came as clearly as a voice, though I didn't think I was hearing it from outside. It simply came to me as though I had heard it. I was enrolled in the pre-Law program of the college, and had collected all the computer cards for the classes in that program. I went back, cancelled them all, and started the Biblical languages program.

I pursued the program in Biblical languages with enthusiasm. I thought that if the Bible was my guide to life, it would be best to know as much as possible about it. Looking back at it, I believe some try for righteousness by works, some by faith, but that I pursued righteousness by Biblical languages. After completing my Bachelor of Arts degree, I went on to graduate school and took a Master of Arts in Religion, still concentrating in Biblical languages. I was learning more and more about the Bible, but my spiritual life was deteriorating at the same time. During four quarters of graduate school I attended church three times. My prayer life was practically non-existent.

I was unwilling to make Christianity a total surrender, which seemed to me a one-way street.

Shortly after completing my MA program I decided not to enter teaching ministry and instead went into the U. S. Air Force. Within another year, I broke officially from the Seventh-day Adventist Church and from any church. My problems were not with specific Seventh-day Adventist doctrines, though I would now dispute some of those. I regard Seventh-day Adventists as fellow-Christians despite any doctrinal disagreements. My rejection of the church and the faith was for reasons that applied equally well to most varieties of Christianity. In particular I could not find an anchor for my faith in an understanding of scripture alone, and I couldn't accept the idea of a total surrender to God without such an anchor. I was unwilling to make Christianity a total surrender, which seemed to me a one-way street. Some Christians argued with me that such a total

3

surrender as I described was not required, but I could not see a partial surrender to God at the time, and I still can't do so. (I will discuss my view of scripture more in the chapter entitled *It has been Written.*)

I stayed out of the church entirely for approximately 12 years. I emphasize the totality of my rejection of the faith. I did not pray, even in some instances when I felt I was about to lose my life. I read the Bible only to keep up my language skills. I refused to attend any church services, except for a brief time at a Unitarian-Universalist congregation. While I did not write anything against the church, I was quite vocal in conversations with friends, and generally less tolerant of Christianity and Christians than those who had grown up with little religion.

I was generally less tolerant of Christianity and Christians than those who had grown up with little religion.

In 1993, I was a partner in a small corporation working on developing game software. I was working 15 or 16 hours daily seven days a week. My work was my life at the time. My business partner was concerned that I was going to burn out, and as I was the sole developer for our small company, this was a matter of serious concern to him. He began to suggest various forms of diversion. I would shoot down each idea as he brought it up. Finally, in desperation, he suggested that since I had "all those Bible degrees" I should try attending church. As a matter of entertainment, I thought that would be interesting. I had grown up in church, but had attended Seventh-day Adventist churches almost exclusively. I had very little knowledge of how any other denominations conducted church services or what they believed.

With a true software engineering approach I made a list of denominations I wanted to check out, then went to the phone book

4

and looked for churches of that denomination to attend. I programmed my search, and knew where I would be going some time in advance.

After a few weeks of this I came to "United Methodist" on my list of denominations. I already had a church selected for that, but the Sunday morning I had planned to attend it found me with a software delivery for the Monday morning following, and the work incomplete. I decided that I had better work Sunday morning until it was finished rather than attend church and count on being able to complete the work in the afternoon. It was probably a good decision, because it was 4:00 PM before the work was done and ready for delivery. I then decided that perhaps I should try an evening service at the church of my choice, but the United Methodist church I had selected did not have an evening service. I went back to the yellow pages and found one that both listed an evening service and had directions I could understand. That church was Pine Forest United Methodist Church.

I truly hated that first evening service. The contemporary style of music annoyed me. Three youth gave testimonies that got on my nerves, about things I would never do.

I truly hated that first evening service. The contemporary style of music annoyed me. Three youth gave testimonies that got on my nerves, about things I would never do. I left pretty much assuming that I would never return there again. Then I got an attack of fairness. I had planned to attend morning services in the various churches I had on my list, but I had given this church only an evening service. (I had done this with one other church and it didn't bother me at all!) I decided I should attend Pine Forest UMC once more for a day time service. I did this the following Sunday.

This started an interesting pattern. I determined each Sunday that I would not continue attending the services, and then each Sunday would find me back. There was a fine group of people in my Sunday School class who took me in immediately and made me feel welcome. They also conducted some interesting free-wheeling discussions which were very enjoyable.

In a few weeks I called the pastor and asked for an official statement of what United Methodists believed. He had some difficulty figuring out what to give me, but finally suggested the United Methodist Discipline. I found the statement of doctrines particularly interesting, especially the section on sources of our faith. This statement is of the Wesleyan quadrilateral, though it doesn't label it as such. It includes the statement that: "Wesley believed that the living core of the Christian faith was revealed in Scripture, illumined by tradition, vivified in personal experience, and confirmed by reason" (United Methodist Discipline, 1992, ¶ 68). This statement owes much to a number of other Christian groups, but it was this particular statement that first struck me and started me on the path back to the church. Many people have asked me why I emphasize this point of doctrine so much. The reason is simple. This is where I began again to bring the living Christ back into my life.

> **"Wesley believed that the living core of the Christian faith was revealed in Scripture, illumined by tradition, vivified in personal experience, and confirmed by reason."**

The reality of the experience of Jesus was something I could take hold of. By itself, experience might be too subjective, but there was the experience of others and that of the community, along with the core experience recorded in scripture. (There is always an

6

element of the subjective in experience; else we would not have *personal* experience.)

There were two important experiences during the time over the six months while I was working my way slowly back into the church.

First, there came the time when I began to read the Bible again, not as a linguistic or literary exercise, but for enlightenment. I have often wondered since this experience whether the devil can tempt one to read the Bible. One evening I was thinking about religion and the church and remembered how much I used to enjoy reading the Bible. So I decided to read some. I started with Hebrews, one of those books I had enjoyed. (Hebrews isn't one of the "introductory" sorts of books, for those who are not well acquainted with scripture.) I began to read and carried on until I reached chapter 6, where I read the following:

For it is impossible to restore again to repentance those who have once been enlightened . . . and then have fallen away.

For it is impossible to restore again to repentance those who have once been enlightened, and have tasted the heavenly gift, and have shared in the Holy Spirit, and have tasted the goodness of the word of God and the powers of the age to come, and then have fallen away, since on their own they are crucifying again the Son of God and are holding him up to contempt.
— Hebrews 6:4-6 (NRSV)

I stopped right there. I read it again.

It still said the same thing.

I thought that perhaps this was one of the reasons why I knew Biblical languages. I could check out translations like these and get things straight! So I took out my Greek New Testament and read the verse in Greek.

It said the same thing.

Well, I thought, perhaps my language skills have deteriorated a bit. I have quite a number of Bible versions in my collection.

So I read the verse in several other versions.

They all said the same thing.

> **To me, at the time, the plain meaning of the text was, "You're lost. Period. No hope."**

I could not think of any interpretation that I wanted to hear, so I even resorted to commentaries. Now several commentaries that I had gave explanations which were pleasant to hear, but all of them sounded to me like they were talking around the plain meaning of the text.

To me, at the time, the plain meaning of the text was, "You're lost. Period. No hope."

So there I was on the bed (I often read lying down) surrounded by Bibles and feeling thoroughly depressed. All my scholarship failed me at that moment. Then one text came to mind: "If we confess our sins, he is faithful and just to forgive us our sins, and to <u>cleanse</u> us from all unrighteousness" 1 John 1:9 (KJV). Yes, I remembered it in the KJV, as I had memorized it. It struck me right then that I didn't need to figure out how to handle Hebrews 6:4-6 right then because I could simply know that I was confessing my sin, and the promise was there that God would forgive. At that moment I knew and experienced God's forgiveness.

My other key experience came during a revival at Pine Forest United Methodist Church, preached by Bishop William Morris of the Alabama-West Florida conference of the UMC. I attended because I thought it was likely that listening to a Methodist bishop was one of the better ways to gather what United Methodists believed. (There may be some doubt about this procedure, but I thought it was pretty good at the time!) It was during the simple but beautiful messages presented by the bishop that I made my decision to return to the church.

I didn't respond immediately, not because I was in doubt about what I was going to do, but because I was in doubt about many theological points and how those would affect my reception by a particular denomination or church congregation. When I finally did return formally to the church, I did so with a promise to the Lord not to allow the views of others to change my relationship to Him. Relationship became first and theology last. I have found this to be a good plan for living with the church. There will always be points which can be doubted. There will always be doctrines that various members will question one another about. But these don't need to be the critical issues.

Fellowship often will have more to do with attracting someone to a church than the preaching or any of the other formal programs.

One of the things that kept me at Pine Forest UMC was my Sunday School class, the Wesleyan Adventurers. The members of that class drew me in, included me, and loved me into their church. I appreciate every one of them. That class no longer exists at Pine Forest due to controversies surrounding the revival at Brownsville

Assembly of God (Pensacola, FL), a situation I regret deeply. What is important, however, is that the personal touch and the fellowship often will have more to do with attracting someone to a church than the preaching or any of the other formal programs. Many churches would do well to consider these simple things in their outreach programs.

I remained at Pine Forest United Methodist Church, and in late 1994 I was involved in starting the Pacesetters Bible School. Pine Forest UMC launched the school and still hosts it, but members of other congregations and other denominations were invited to participate. I became director of the school. I worked along with the church staff through the interesting period of revival in the local area, but I stood back from many of the active details. I would teach, but I would rarely participate in altar prayer times or other such events.

As I began to pray for some of the college age youth of the church, I was stopped.

In August of 1998, the Lord took me on, so to speak, in my office. It was a week during which I expected to be particularly productive. Pastor Perry Dalton was leading a mission trip in Costa Rica and very little was planned here in the way of activities. On Tuesday morning I came late to my time of personal prayer. I had been running around and was frustrated at the number of things which could get in the way even during a light week. In a perfunctory fashion I began to pray for my mental lists of people. I'm fairly good with lists. As I began to pray for some of the college age youth of the church, I was stopped. I did not precisely hear a voice, but the words were as clear—and as clearly not mine—as though it was a voice. I believe the Lord was speaking to me, to interrupt me and get me to take my ministry much deeper.

10

In four days of argument with the Lord I got nothing done—the conclusion was simply that I had to be prepared not just to mention names in prayer, but to bear these peoples' burdens before the Lord. Included was a call to intercession, but also a call to a greater concern for the experience of those I taught. It was not a time of correction for my doctrinal beliefs, but a call to application of those beliefs; a call to live up to what I taught.

Since then I have spent much more of my time in prayer, and much more of my teaching time in teaching about prayer. The key lesson I learned from this August experience was simply that the Lord continuously calls us to move in closer and to become more real in our ministry and in our activity.

Finally, I heard the Lord say, "I have already told you who in this church has the gifts and insights on this issue. Ask her! I'm not going to tell you."

I'd like to tell you, and I'm sure you'd like to see that as I became closer to God the troubles stopped. But that isn't true. Since that time, I have experienced both great joy and considerable hardship. I don't try to rank hardships, and neither should you. I found my particular set of hardships very difficult to bear. But God has continued to sustain me and to teach me through all of them.

One of the joys I experienced came in November of 1999 as I was married and acquired a family and even a grandchild at age 42. A year before, the Lord had led me to my wife-to-be, Jody Webb, who was a prayer warrior in our church, and particularly in individual prayer ministry. The Lord first directed me to her to hear her thoughts and ideas regarding prayer. I was working with a city-wide prayer movement at the time, and following one of our prayer meetings I was troubled by a number of things that had happened. I prayed earnestly about the problem but didn't get any guidance or understanding.

Finally, I heard the Lord say, "I have already told you who in this church has the gifts and insights on this issue. Ask her! I'm not going to tell you." I must note here that I never get these wonderful revelations from God that some people report—when I hear from God it's usually a shove in the right direction.

So I went right then and asked her, and indeed she did have insights into that prayer meeting and I did find it enlightening. I did believe that I got guidance from the Lord through that contact.

People who claim to speak for God should remember this. The hearer is also someone who can listen to the Spirit of God and can and must discern.

Later, I felt the Lord leading me to seek a closer relationship with this lady. I'm going to discuss discernment and knowing when God is speaking and what God is saying to *you* in a later chapter. Right here I want to say something about hearing from the Lord about things that involve another person's life. Your words from the Lord about how you should behave should never become the means of pressuring or putting another person on the spot. I felt more strongly than I had ever felt anything in my life that I should court Jody. But I also knew that she had to follow her judgment and what she heard from the Lord. I believe that I always framed my conversations in such a way that I was not using any claim of the Lord speaking to me as pressure on her.

People who claim to speak for God should remember this. The hearer is also someone who can listen to the Spirit of God and can and must discern. God's word is always true, but it never comes labeled with safety warnings. Each person must discern. It is more like one person getting an insight and letting others seek their understanding of it.

When we got engaged, I followed the same principles. I had been praying for over a week. When I spoke to her about it, instead of asking her and expecting an immediate answer, I told her that I had been praying about it, but that she should have as much opportunity as she desired to hear from God for herself. I offered her my commitment, but did not give any time frame. I said I was not going to bring it up again. She would just have to get her timing from God.

It took about a week. That was quite a week of waiting. I had felt God's leading to ask, but I had not felt any kind of "prediction" form God as to how things would proceed. At the time her son—soon to be our son—was in treatment for cancer. There were plenty of reasons why she (and I, for that matter) wouldn't want to add complications to our lives. But God led, and God provided, and we were married.

When James passed on we felt the presence of God in the room.

The major of sorrow my life over the last five years came with the major sorrow. Our son James was 12 years old when he was diagnosed. Over time, our relationship grew very close, but those five years were punctuated by episodes with cancer treatment, and finally, in September of 2004, with his death. But there was a peace and even a joy involved there too. As James knew he was about to go, he called for his family, and we called for his closest friends who played in the praise band with him. They gathered around, pulled out the guitars and sang. My wife read some favorite scriptures to him as various ones of us gathered around. He passed on peacefully, and we felt the presence of God in the room.

Some people believe that we must receive physical healing in order for God to be present and involved. But James, at 17 years of age, was able to accept what was happening to him, and to live as a witness of courage. His high school band has named an award for excellence in percussion performance after him. His church is collecting money to create a multimedia studio in his name and based on his plans. There is a golf tournament that raises money for children with cancer that was inspired by his actions. His deeds keep following him.

I want to make it clear that the joy doesn't eliminate the sorrow. Many people think that the hope of heaven, and the good things

I believe with all my heart that God leads and acts in the present.

accomplished by a person in life ought to eliminate the sorrow of death. They do help bear it. They do help us move on with our lives, but they don't make the cancer a good thing. They just make some good out of a very bad experience.

As I write this I'm focusing my teaching ministry on small groups, the internet, and writing. I believe with all my heart that God leads and acts in the present. You're going to read a number of my thoughts and my understanding of how God acts and how we should act in this book.

Many people have a problem associating the parts of me they call "liberal" with the parts of me they call "conservative" and those they call "charismatic." I'm not particularly interested in making the labels work together. I'm not willing to argue much about labels. I believe firmly in Jesus Christ as my savior and Lord. I believe that he commanded me to love, and that the love he commands makes me reach out to everyone openly, honestly and without judgment. I believe that he works every day and that there

14

is nothing God was willing to do in the days of the apostles that he is not willing to do today.

Some find my statement that Jesus is my savior and Lord impossible to reconcile with my pursuit of dialogue. Some find my focus on scripture impossible to reconcile with my view that God speaks today, and that God's gifts continue. I'm sorry if I scramble your labels—No I'm not!! I think your labels need scrambling.

If you don't want them scrambled, don't read this book!

Have the same attitude of mind that Jesus had,

Though he was in the divine form,
He did cling to his equality with God,
> *But he emptied himself,*
> *Taking the form of a slave,*
> *Becoming human in form,*
>> *And being found in human pattern,*
>>> *He became obedient to death,*
>>>> ***Even death on a cross,***
>>> *So God has exalted him,*
>>> *And given him a name above all names,*
>> *So that at the name of Jesus every knee should bow*
>> *Heavenly, earthly and beneath the earth,*
>> *And every tongue should confess*
That Jesus Christ is Lord
To the glory of the Father

— Philippians 2:5-11

I Am Not Ashamed

There might be many reasons why someone would be ashamed of the good news about God that is represented in what we call the "gospel."

Historically, the shame was in worshipping a convicted and executed criminal, calling him God and following his teachings. Very few people doubt that Jesus died, and that he was executed by the barbaric method of crucifixion. Raised from the dead, alive today—that's another matter entirely. But the death is the best established thing about Jesus. I've entered into debates about whether such a person as Jesus existed historically. All of these debates start—must start—with a list of things that I will demonstrate limiting myself strictly to the tools of a historian, to the extent that past events can be demonstrated. These are the things that Jesus did or that happened to him. Many scholars have created such lists. Invariably, "crucified by the Romans" is on them. Jesus' death by crucifixion is as established as a historical fact gets.

We know the crucifixion is a horrible thing, but the symbols involved in it have become commonplace and familiar, and they are objects involved in the rituals of the church, not in execution.

It seems remote and distant to us. If we have shame in anything about Jesus or Christianity, it is something different than it was for Paul and other early disciples. For us, the cross is the symbol of a religion, a person, or a faith system. We see it on churches every

17

day. We have pictures of crosses, sometimes with a figure of Jesus hanging on them. Sometimes the figure will be portrayed with a halo. We make earrings and necklaces with crosses. We know the crucifixion is a horrible thing, but the symbols involved in it have become commonplace and familiar, and they are objects involved in the rituals of the church, not in execution.

We may be ashamed of some of the people who carry crosses, or of some of the groups that worship in buildings with crosses on them. We may object to where crosses are placed, such as on the lawns of public buildings. But none of this is quite what the "shame of the cross" would have been for the early followers of Jesus.

There was a shame in worshipping someone who had been crucified.

Put yourself back in Paul's time. Jesus was recently executed. The one political power in the world was the authority by which that execution was carried out. That particular form of execution was one reserved for the worst, and especially for rebels and political offenders. There was a shame in worshipping someone who had been crucified. It had the aura and the stigma of worshipping a mass murderer, perhaps a bit like modern Americans would feel about a cult worshipping Charles Manson.

But in addition, it was something dangerous. The followers of Jesus were proclaiming as divine someone executed by the Roman authorities. Divinity was being carried by someone who was a rebel and a dangerous character. Proclaiming the kingdom of a rebel was an act of rebellion in and of itself.

And here we have Paul proclaiming that he is not ashamed of this good news. He glories in the cross, glories in an instrument of shame. In disaster, he finds good news.

One of the key elements of that good news lies in the fact that you see a cross with much different emotions than did the people of Paul's day. That element is transformation. The symbol of the cross has been transformed from one of disaster, death, agony, shame, and despair into one of hope for many people. Not all people, and we'll discuss that as well.

That transformation comes from the way in which God used the experience of the cross. God came to the earth in the human form of Jesus. God experienced life with us. He took action as we might need to take action under the circumstances of our lives. He found himself in an occupied country, living under cruel foreign domination. He didn't just come and appear on a mountaintop. He got involved in human experiences, human emotions, human weaknesses, and yes, human strengths as well. When it came down to it, he died a death in just the way that a human would have to do it in that time and place.

When it came down to it, he died a death in just the way that a human would have to do it in that time and place.

The first part, then, of the transformation was involvement. The cross would never have been transformed as a symbol without the involvement. God, the infinite gap-crosser, crossed the gap and stayed on our side long enough to experience the worst of the worst.

But not only did he get involved, he stayed involved. The second part of that transformation was endurance. God didn't quit. He carried through. If he had not, we could think of the wonderful time when God was with people, lived with us, talked with us, worked with us, but we would always have a distance from him, because he would never have experienced the one thing that seems to terrify most of us—death. "Through death, he destroyed the one who had the power of death" (Hebrews 2:14). "He endured the cross; he treated the shame with contempt" (Hebrews 12:2).

Jesus knew when to ignore what others thought was shame. The shame was intended to fall on the one who was punished. But Jesus had no reason to be ashamed and he knew it. Knowing what one should ignore is an important part of living in this imperfect world. Many people, Christians and others, have endured torture and death with dignity and even peace because they knew this lesson. What was intended to bring shame on them instead became a source of glory.

The transformation that Jesus accomplished on the cross, symbolized by the transformation of the cross itself, is something that we all can grasp. Circumstances and our environment are not fixed things that we have to take as they are. They can be transformed by our attitude and by the way that we deal with them. Every cross in your life, everything that you would prefer not to have done or not to have encountered can be transformed. When we give testimonies of things that have happened to us, this is what we are doing.

If you are focusing on the darkness, and the negative things that have happened, perhaps you haven't let those things be transformed yet.

Some think that testimony meetings are about telling how dark our lives were before God intervened. And sometimes they are. But if you are focusing on the darkness, and the negative things that have happened, perhaps you haven't let those things be transformed yet. Did you become involved, stay involved, and endure? Did you have contempt for the supposed shame? The real point of a testimony, a witness, is to present how things have changed, not how much they are the same.

20

But there's one more part of this process. Some of you may be wondering whether I'm going to ignore it.

Jesus triumphed over the adversity. He rose again from the dead. His movement should have died. It came back to life. Without this, the transformation could not have taken place. In this sense, only one who was God, or totally in tune with God's spirit, could have triumphed. We daily deal with circumstances and troubles. Jesus was dealing with the nastiest circumstance of all—death. He was there to deny and destroy the one who had the power over death.

I'm not going to argue here about the physical resurrection of Jesus. It's very hard, if not impossible to prove a miracle. But I do think the greatest evidence that something different happened that day in Palestine is that the movement surrounding Jesus didn't go away. Having seen Jesus crucified, his movement should have failed, but it didn't.

The critical element in transforming the symbol of the cross from one of shame to one of hope and glory was simply that the followers of Jesus *believed* that he had conquered death.

But the critical element in transforming the symbol of the cross from one of shame to one of hope and glory was simply that the followers of Jesus *believed* that he had conquered death. You may debate me about the idea that without something special happening on the morning of the resurrection, the followers of Jesus would simply have scattered. You may have another explanation you think works as well. But I think there can be no doubt that unless the followers of Jesus *believed* that something had happened, there would have been no transformation, no Jesus movement, no Christianity, and the cross would forever have remained a symbol of shame, or passed into history as an example of the barbarism of ancient cultures.

But the fact is that those followers *did* believe, they didn't scatter, but continued to proclaim the victory of the person the Romans had crucified. And it was in that proclamation that the cross was transformed.

Jesus could have died with dignity, endured the shame, and risen from the dead, but if nobody had arisen to proclaim those facts, no transformation would have taken place. It took human beings getting involved, carrying the message, and *acting* on the good news. I'm sometimes accused of being very human oriented in my religious beliefs. But I believe that this orientation toward what people do and how they respond is thoroughly Biblical. Not only did God accomplish reconciliation through Christ, but he gave us the same ministry. In other words, God knows and intends the human element to be critical in carrying out his mission on earth.

God knows and intends the human element to be critical in carrying out his mission on earth.

And that leads to the other side of the issue of shame. We need to be prepared to deny the shame just as Jesus did on the cross. But we also need to be able to see shame when it's appropriate. A great deal of who we are and how we live will be determined by our response to shame.

In Ezekiel 9 we have a part of a vision of Ezekiel. The prophet has been shown abominations that the Israelites are committing right in the temple precincts. Then a man is sent out in the city to make a mark on certain people. The ones who are marked are those who "sign and cry" about the abominations committed in the land (Ezekiel 9:4). (I like the good old KJV "sigh and cry" because the

22

Hebrew words involved here are alliterative). Then others are told to follow and slaughter everyone who is not marked. Notice that it is not the ones who themselves are not committing abominations, but those who are deeply bothered by the evil things that are going on.

I have seen this passage turned outward many times, as though it is a call to Christians to sigh and cry about the abominations committed by everyone else. But we should remember that this passage was written by an Israelite prophet to Israelites. If we are going to transfer it to Christians we need to transfer it all the way. It isn't speaking to Christians about their attitude toward the actions of non-Christians, but rather about their reaction to their own abominations.

I said that the cross was a symbol of hope for some. But it's a symbol of death and destruction for others. It becomes a symbol of shame again when those who proclaim it use it in shameful ways. The crusades, the inquisition, the holocaust—all were justified at some point by reference to Christianity and to the cross. All too often, others did not stand against those who abused the cross, and did not proclaim its true meaning. We can choose either to restore the cross again as a symbol of hope, or we can use it as a symbol of hostility, destruction, and death. In order to restore the cross to the glory of Christ's transformation, we need to get to the point where we sigh and cry for the abominations committed by Christians.

The cross becomes a symbol of shame again when those who proclaim it use it in shameful ways. The crusades, the inquisition, the holocaust—all were justified at some point by reference to Christianity and to the cross.

I was involved in a program a few years back in which we had an opportunity to write statements about ourselves on sticky notes, stick them to our shirts, and then engage others in the group in conversation based on what was written on their notes. I included "Christian," "individual liberty," and "no coercion" amongst the items on my list. Several people thought this was a surprising combination. To them, Christianity stood for compulsion, force, and tyranny. How could I be both a Christian and an advocate of liberty? I wish I could blame the problem on their prejudice, on their misconception of what Christians are. But too often Christians behave in a way that is completely the opposite of the principles Jesus taught, and totally incompatible with the way he behaved. At the same time, *other Christians are silent.* We need to be ashamed of what is truly shameful, and proud of what is worthy of pride.

In the cross, God displayed his willingness to cross the gap and communicate with us where we are.

The answer lies in the symbolism of the cross. In the cross, God displayed his willingness to cross the gap and communicate with us where we are. He endured the force. He was subject to the compulsion. He was executed by the existing tyrants. In so doing he gave an example of liberation.

But many of his followers have missed the message. They have decided that Jesus was so right that anyone who disagreed with him had to be forced into right thinking. They inverted the message, making Jesus into the tyrant and the torturer. If you really think about what happened on the cross, I think it will become terribly clear what a horrible reversal this is. Too often Christians have sided with the soldiers driving in the nails.

So how do I respond to these things done in the name of Jesus? I'm quick to say that this is not what Jesus taught. But I reject the notion of telling other people that those who did this were not

24

"real" Christians. I may even believe that in my heart, but if I defend myself by that means, I force others into deciding who is and who is not a real Christian. It's likely that they won't take on the task.

What I have to do is acknowledge the wrongs that have been done, and testify to the transformation that Jesus intended. I need to sigh and cry—I need to specifically, openly, and sincerely denounce the shameful actions of my fellow Christians, and do so without distancing myself, without setting myself up as the one true Christian and good guy. I only compound the problem when I try to make others sort one Christian out from another. That is not their task. This is the time to acknowledge the problem.

As we continue in the same tradition, we need to deal with the things that have happened in what is now, for good or bad, our history.

Please notice carefully that I say we need to denounce the *actions*. We deal with the fruit, not the people. Let God deal with the people. Gossiping is not sighing and crying, even if you do it with a whiny voice! Make sure that what you are sighing and crying about is an abomination. I have heard sighing and crying in the church about everything from minor discomforts and annoyances to personal preferences. In fact, we are much more likely to sigh and cry about our comfort than about real abominations.

Christian readers may protest that they, as Christians, did not do any of these things. That is very likely true. But they were done in the name of Jesus, they were done in the name of the same faith, and they were often done without protest, or without adequate protest from other Christians. As we continue in the same tradition, we need to deal with the things that have happened in what is now, for good or bad, our history.

25

Why should Christians take on such a burden? *Because we are the ones who know the power of transformation.* We are the ones who worship the crucified one. We are the ones who can make a difference if we will truly follow the one who transformed the cross from despair into hope.

And we need not be ashamed of *that*!

Of the Good News

Sometimes it's hard to find the good news in what happens in Christian churches from week to week. We see a building filled with people who feel it's their duty to be there, or who are there to socialize, and they go through a set of rituals that they know is church because that's the way they grew up. Between services there is the wrangling of committee meetings and debates with the pastor over how the church is run.

It's no wonder that so few Christians want to share their faith, and when they do, that they do it so poorly and in such an unconvincing way. Sometimes the non-Christian gets the impression that what we Christians think of as "good news" is the idea that I'm a truly horrible sinner, and the solution is for me to go to church every Sunday and pay tithe!

Sometimes the non-Christian gets the impression that what we Christians think of as "good news" is the idea that I'm a truly horrible sinner, and the solution is for me to go to church every Sunday and pay tithe!

(Don't get the idea that I'm against tithe here. One key to carrying out God's mission in the world is stewardship of all the resources he provides.)

I know that's a caricature that is very unfair to many readers. But it isn't too far from the truth in many churches. And then the members and pastors wonder why the church doesn't grow and can never meet its bills.

27

But it's not totally unfair to everyone. And there is a further view of "good news" that I think is true of many, many more believers, and in this case very often sincere, enthusiastic, and active Christians. This is the view that the good news is essentially about theology and doctrine. I'm often asked, "What is it that I have to teach someone, what is it that I have to get someone to believe, in order to be sure that they are saved?" The usual answer, in many tracts and books on sharing one's faith goes something like this:

1. Convince the person of their sinfulness
2. Convince them that they are unable to help themselves
3. Convince them that the Bible is true
4. Convince them that the Bible says Jesus died for their sins and paid the penalty.
5. Convince them to put their trust in Jesus and in his substitutionary sacrifice.
6. Have them pray the sinner's prayer, telling God all of that.
7. Tell them that now they're no longer going to hell.

"Just as the Father sent me, I'm sending you!"
– Jesus

Now I don't really want to make fun of this approach that is so time tested, but I do want us to look at some serious flaws in it. It seems to me that the person who is approached in this fashion needs to learn a good deal of theology before they can receive the good news. Instead of going to church and paying tithe, the solution is in understanding theological concepts and getting some doctrinal positions right.

Some of this we might blame on Paul. A great deal of our witnessing comes from his writings. But I don't think the problem is really Paul's fault. We need to recognize that Paul wrote his letters to churches, largely ones he had already witnessed to, and to leaders who were under his guidance. Paul was explaining the Christian life and walk to people who were already Christians.

I want to make clear here that I'm not saying that Paul was writing theology either. I believe that many major problems with Christian doctrine result from reading Paul as a theologian. He was an apostle and a pastor. He wrote pastoral letters. When he was making theological points he was trying to help Christians develop their Christian walk, endure in it, and learn to proclaim it.

But let's turn to Jesus for an example of witness. Jesus said, "Just as the Father sent me, I'm sending you" John 20:21. But what does that mean?

I think it means much the same thing as Paul was saying in 1 Corinthians. Jesus came bringing reconciliation, and he sends us out to do the same thing. Jesus approached people with healing. He means us to do the same thing. Jesus gave people hope. He wants us to do the same thing. Jesus made people who were miserable feel better. He wants us to do the same thing.

Jesus came bringing reconciliation and he sends us out to do the same thing.

I challenge you to find where Jesus tried to convince people that they were miserable sinners. He did say that they needed to put their trust in him. I challenge you to find where he taught anybody the theology of salvation and asked them to accept it. He didn't. He did call for their trust and promise them that he would be faithful.

The good news of the gospel is not about how miserable you are or were. It's not about doctrines like original sin, justification, sanctification, imputed or imparted righteousness, or realized versus unrealized eschatology. The good news about the gospel says that God loves you, cares for you, respects you, wants a relationship with you, and is willing to provide for your spiritual healing and future, just as he created and upholds the universe. God is willing to go to extreme lengths to bring you to him, to make you understand his love and care. That's good news.

Doctrines and theological systems can attempt to describe the reality. Church worship services can celebrate it. Giving, such as in tithing, can grow from it. Understanding can result from living it. But none of these things are actually the good news.

> **Doctrines and theological systems can attempt to describe the reality. Church worship services can celebrate it. Giving, such as in tithing, can grow from it. Understanding can result from living it. But none of these things are actually the good news.**

Bottom line:

✓ **God loves you.**
What that means is that he puts a value on you and will go out of his way, even to the extent of experiencing death on the cross, to get you to understand that love

✓ **God cares for you.**
We complain of the difficulties of the world, but we cannot imagine what it would be like to live in a world that didn't follow natural laws. God's power is demonstrated on a daily basis.

✓ **God respects you.**
Some of my more theologically inclined friends may be questioning this one, but God created humanity a little bit less than God (Psalm 8:4), and he allows human beings to make their own choices and plot their own course. He *tries* to communicate, but he doesn't force communication.

30

✓ **God wants a relationship with you.**
This follows from the preceding points. The efforts that God makes lead to a relationship. Otherwise they make no sense.

✓ **God provides for your spiritual needs and future.**
We greatly underestimate the importance of this. But those who see life as futile either give up or live lives of quiet despair. But God is the provider of spiritual needs as well.

✓ **God goes to extreme lengths to bring us to him.**
Within the limitations of respect, God does everything he can to lead us in his direction. I believe that there are many who aren't even aware of it who are nonetheless led toward God, and that they demonstrate this through loving one another. Often those who don't claim to belong to God's kingdom live better kingdom lives than those who do!

I haven't taken the time here to try to prove any of these points, either scripturally or logically. I will discuss some of them later in this book. But here I'm just sharing how I understand the message of Jesus.

Everyone who loves has experienced divine birth, and knows God.
— 1 John 4:20

But how should these points work themselves out into the lives of followers of Jesus? Let me suggest some ideas:

✓ **They show themselves in love.**
"Loved ones, if God loved us this way, we ought to love each other too" 1 John 4:11. The result of receiving God's love is love for one another.

✓ **They require that we place love first.**
This is controversial, because there are so many Biblical tests of doctrines and teachings. But I will suggest that God-like love is the first test. "Loved ones, Love one

31

another, because love is from God. Everyone who loves has experienced divine birth, and knows God. Anyone who doesn't love doesn't know God, for God is love" 1 John 4:7-8. The heretic under torture knew God better than the inquisitor, no matter how wrong or right doctrinally either of them was.

✓ **They require that we seek relationships.**
Lonely Christianity is not an option. I don't mean routine church services each week with formal greetings in the few minutes provided by the order of service. I'm suggesting long term, deep relationships with people you care about and who care about you. I mean seeking relationships where you don't have them. I mean seeking relationships without an ulterior motive. Don't go out making relationships in the hopes that the person will go to church with you and become a Christian. Seek relationships because you care, and because you enjoy that God-like activity. You are never more God-like than when you open your heart's door to another person. The more different they are, the more God-like that action is.

> **You are never more God-like than when you open your heart's door to another person. The more different they are, the more God-like that action is.**

✓ **They require that we treat others with respect.**
God respects our choices, even when they are totally wrong and destructive. This is something that is very hard to grasp, because it seems to us that it would be so much better for God to protect us completely from hardship. But God respects our choices instead. As a parent of a teenager, this was very difficult for me. How can one allow the teenager to make choices, especially ones that you know are going to hurt? Can you

32

stop him from experiencing the results of his choices? Sadly, but correctly, you cannot.

✓ **They require that we be willing to go to extremes.**
I like to call myself a passionate moderate, and going to extremes is something that I don't find easy to do. When I do feel that I'm on an extreme, I start to defend myself. But Jesus was willing to go to the extreme of death on the cross to open a relationship with us. He was willing to be despised for the people he associated with. But he didn't let it bother him. He kept right on moving. I've experienced condemnation for people that I associate with, but I must admit that I am nowhere nearly as willing to be at the wrong place according to popular opinion as Jesus was. But that's the divine example we have been given.

If you live like Jesus did you might be considered a wimp, a collaborator, a drunkard, or an immoral person.

How could someone be ashamed of such a program? Why do Paul and I both feel the need to proclaim, "I am not ashamed?"

The shame lies in the common view, in how the person who really proclaims love is perceived. If you live like Jesus did you might be considered a wimp, a collaborator, a drunkard, or an immoral person. You might even be considered a danger to society because you encourage that kind of people.

But followers of Jesus take up the mission of transformation—transformation of symbols, transformation of relationships, and transformation of people.

And there's nothing to be ashamed of in *that*!

³How then shall we escape after neglecting such a tremendous deliverance? The Lord spoke of this deliverance first, then it was confirmed to us by those who heard him. ⁴God also confirmed their testimony with signs and wonders and various powerful deeds, and with the Holy Spirit apportioned according to his will.

— Hebrews 2:3-4

For it is God's Power

"Whatever Happened to the Power of God?" is the title of a book by Michael Brown. With all apologies to Dr. Brown (and I very much enjoyed reading his book), God's power is precisely where it always has been. The question I have to ask is: "Do we recognize God's power when we see it?"

Now I know if I was saying this to an audience in person, there would be some hands in the air (I always encourage questions) ready to tell me that I'm not really quite getting the question. The power that people are looking for is the same power that made the sun stand still, that brought down fire from heaven to consume Elijah's sacrifice, or called Lazarus out of the tomb. That's the power of God that people are wondering about. Why aren't things like that happening any more? "What kind of 'power of God' are you talking about?" they ask.

I believe we are all living in a big miracle.

I'm talking about the power that created and sustains the universe—the power that is allowing me to take another breath so that I can continue to write this book.

You see, I believe we are all living in a big miracle. The miracle takes the form of the universe around us. God created it, and God sustains it. He doesn't do this by adding power to it from a distance, or commanding special events from his far away throne. Rather, he "carries it by his powerful word" (Hebrews 1:3) and does so all the time, consistently.

35

This is the primary demonstration of God's power. The Bible starts with the creation, and ends with the new creation. God is the creator. That's primarily what he does. As long as there is stuff, and there are people to see the stuff, God's power is being demonstrated.

"But we're talking about God's supernatural power," someone complains. "We're not talking about the ordinary stuff that goes on every day." Just try to live without the ordinary stuff and see how you feel about that. Oops! You won't exist any more without the ordinary stuff. While we live in a big miracle all the time, we wonder about all the little miracles.

Why intervene for Joshua by making the sun stand still and not send miraculous hordes against the Nazis?

On the other hand there are those who think that God cannot intervene in any manner other than the ordinary consistent way in which he sustains the universe without being unfair. Solve one problem. Why intervene for Joshua by making the sun stand still and not send miraculous hordes against the Nazis?

That's a tough question. But before I answer it, let's take a look at this business of supernatural, natural and how God acts.

The Hand of God[1]

It was a fine Easter Sunday morning, but my Sunday School class was focused on disaster. A week earlier, during Palm Sunday services, a church in neighboring Alabama had been hit by a tornado. A number of church members were killed, including the pastor's four year old daughter. The expected questions were flying around the table. "Couldn't God protect his church?" "Why would God allow such a thing to happen?" Nobody in the room thought it was a judgment of God, but some were certain they had neighbors who would wonder what sin the congregation had committed to merit such punishment.

When people see acts of God and miracles, they say, "God is active. God is showing his power." When there are few such acts, they perceive God as distant or inactive. "Why doesn't God do something?" they ask.

> **Why would God intervene in one case and not in another?**

But such acts, in most people's view, need explanations. Why would God intervene in one case and not in another? Shouldn't God always intervene to accomplish the good? Why do we hear about so many minor interventions (at least apparent ones) but we can't find major interventions in many cases in which we think they should occur, such as for the victims of Hitler or Stalin?

I think there is a fundamental problem with this view of God and the universe. If God is involved in the universe at all, I would suspect he is always involved. Perhaps some time I will write

---

[1] The majority of the material in this section was taken from my three part series of essays, previously published on Enerigon.com, entitled The Hand of God.

about why I believe this to be true, but right now let me just say that I think that the whole notion of the God that I have described above seems intensely limiting, demeaning, and anthropomorphic. He is God made in our image. As a human being, I sort tasks much as I described above. I might set my compiler to compiling, and work in another window writing code. The first I have automated (or rather purchased the means for automation), and it can run on its own; the second is beyond my capability to automate. I note this morning that my wife has put in a load of washing, and has then gone to her computer to work on her book. The one is set up to operate automatically, or with minimum intervention; the latter only she can do.

I believe we have divided God's activities along that same line. **God is limited in our minds, and divides and prioritizes his tasks just like we do.** If God can't save the lives of every child in the children's hospital, how can he get involved in trivial affairs as people claim every day—from finding a parking place to arranging a raise? Believe me, I have felt inclined, when my son was in the hospital, to ask these very questions, even though I don't accept the premise on which they are based. It's a very human thing to do.

I have an illustration I use in class to generate questions on this issue. I begin dropping my pen repeated on the desk or podium. When someone asks me why I'm doing that, I ask, "Why does the pen fall?" Inevitably the answer will be something like, "because things fall" or "gravity." "No," I say, "It falls because God wants it to."

Why does God care about something as trivial as the falling of my pen? Well, he does and he doesn't. God wants my pen to fall. That

38

"want" is expressed in the law of gravity. God wants things to behave in that particular way. To divide it into a general law of gravity or a specific desire to influence the actions of my pen is to look at it from a distinctly human, finite perspective.

Does God like bacteria or doesn't he? We see this question most commonly from the perspective of someone who is sick. I have a cold right now. Did God want me to have a cold? Well, by the analogy of my falling pen he certainly did. That "want" was expressed in the form of various aspects of the cycle of life, including bacteria and viruses, which have vital roles to play in our every day lives. Again, dividing that want into the specific desire for me to have a cold, versus the broader desire to have life work in a particular way, is the fundamentally human way of looking at it. I have the cold, so I'm tempted to think of it that way! (If you think the analogy is not fully accurate, consider that the same "want" that causes my pen to fall would participate in causing my death should I fall from a high cliff.)

Do we expect an alteration in the course of nature simply for the purpose of making our lives more pleasant?

How does that relate to hurricanes and tornados? Well, there are particular natural causes which bring about these weather events, and there are benefits as well as costs involved in their passing. We tend to think of them solely in terms of the danger, but nature is renewed through the passing of such storms. We get in the way, and our lives are inconvenienced, tragically altered or even terminated. But do we expect an alteration in the course of nature simply for the purpose of making our lives more pleasant? God didn't sneak the weather up on us by surprise. I knew, for example, when I moved to the Florida gulf coast that I might experience hurricanes. When a hurricane duly showed up, I could curse at God. An atheist could curse nature or circumstances. We'd both be equally silly. What did we expect? Nobody snuck up in the middle of the night, moved the Atlantic Ocean and the Gulf of Mexico out there and then invented hurricanes!

I suspect that building quality, normal weather patterns and good or bad sense had much more to do with the incidents that I described at the beginning of this essay than any particular plan. To look at it from the human point of view God didn't specifically desire that a community in Louisiana be homeless but still have a church, or that a congregation in Alabama have members killed during Palm Sunday services. But it did happen within his will, and according to his rules.

Everything is an act of God, and everything is natural. I believe that this idea of constant, consistent interaction is much closer to an accurate description of how the universe operates than the natural-supernatural dichotomy I described above. The reason is simply that this is what we observe. We would be unable to do science if God intervened on a regular, individually tailored basis. No laws could be stated for gravity, because we would have to know God's attitude toward the particular circumstances.

So everything is an act of God, and everything is natural. But can God intervene in a special way? Does this question make sense? Does it leave any room for divine intervention or is everything simply the result of general laws? Is there anything personal about the universe at all?

However we define God's actions, if God acts in a special way, apart from generalized laws that always work in the same way, we raise the same sort of problems. There are a number of objections to the notion of miracles. Let's look at a few of these briefly.

1. They are impossible. This is true by any standards available to our study. We would hardly be referring to an event as a miracle if it did not in some way contravene the way in which we expected things to happen. But this is hardly, in and of itself, an objection to the possibility of miraculous events. If there is a God who acts, and desires to act at times in an unpredictable ways, it seems unlikely that he would be unable to do so.

2. They are unfair. This problem goes right back to the beginning of my previous essay. Why would God preserve a church, but not the homes of the church members? Why would God permit the death of a pastor's four year old daughter during the course of a church service? Why would God heal one person and not another? These are "why questions" that those of us who believe that God is active in the world often don't want to face.

    Miracles are, by nature, impossible to prove.

3. They are infrequent and difficult if not impossible to prove. If they were frequent we would likely not call them miracles. They would become susceptible to study and definition and would simply become natural laws. That they are difficult to prove is simply a function of their being unusual and infrequent. And even if the event itself is provable, how can one possibly prove intervention of God? Wouldn't simple action of some process or law of which we are unaware be more likely?

I will suggest here that miracles are, by nature, impossible to prove. I'm not going to go into depth on that topic here, but briefly, I believe there are two reasons that combine to make proof impossible. First, all history—all events in the past—are known only to a degree of probability. Many events are known to such a high degree of probability that we can consider them certain for practical purposes. But miracles are by nature unlikely (or impossible) events, and thus certainty is difficult to attain. Consider this: If you were presented with evidence showing that someone had been buried, and then that the tomb had been found empty, would your first supposition be that someone had been raised from the dead, or that someone had removed the body. Yet every Easter Sunday morning I proclaim the more improbable event! Second, we do not know all natural laws. There is no reason to assume that we are aware of all natural processes in the universe. Thus, when something unexpected happens, we cannot be rationally certain that it is not the result of some cause of which we are as yet unaware. This is especially true in the case of healing claims. My father, a missionary, was diagnosed with particular intestinal disease following a surgery. The lab report on a biopsy following surgery confirmed the diagnosis. More than 10 years later, another surgery was needed, and though they found some other work to do, there was no sign that he had ever had the previously diagnosed syndrome. The surgeon said that if he didn't have it now, he never had it. That is quite possible. We don't even have the documentation of the first lab work. The surgeons then were quite convinced. I would add to the second surgeon's statement the words "spontaneous remission"—he got over it and we don't know why! There is a process of healing for this disease, of which we were previously unaware, and yes, a miracle. But proof? I don't see how!

But now back to our central topic. None of these items really answer our central question. They just temporarily set aside some related issues.

42

If God likes to operate the universe according to general and reliable laws (and we observe that this is how the universe operates) is there any room for divine intervention?

In order to suggest an answer to this question I would first like to discuss miracle claims. I do not differentiate between the miracle claims of various religions for this purpose. If all the claims of all the religions of the world were to be allowed as historical, there would actually be very, very little impact on the general course of events in the world. In fact, one remarkable thing about miracles as claimed by any religion is that they seem generally to have very little broad impact on the operation of the physical universe. (Note here that I speak in the physical sense, not in the realm of ideas. The resurrection of Jesus, if historical, had little physical impact, but it has had great ideological impact, no matter how one rates it historically.) But one person being raised from the dead was not enough to make it appear "normal."

If all the claims of all the religions of the world were to be allowed as historical, there would actually be very, very little impact on the general course of events in the world.

A good literary example of this understanding of miracles is found in "The Iliad" in which Homer provides constant examples of divine intervention which always seem to keep the war going more or less the way it would go through human effort.

But there are different varieties of miracle claims. Let me divide these into three major categories:

1. Communication. This variety of miracle simply claims divine communication, that God (or any divine being) has communicated with some person or other. This does not

43

conflict with any natural law, though it goes beyond such law. If it is a process open to all, and not just to certain favored ones, it also is not necessarily unfair. There may simply be certain circumstances under which someone can receive communications from God. I include in this any sort of communication which is received only by the one person. A physical voice which could be heard by anyone in the room would be, in my view, a physical miracle.

2. Arrangements of circumstances. In this case a series of events which are in themselves unremarkable occur in some very remarkable coincidence. We often refer to these as "providential." The preservation of the Bible in so many copies is often called providential because no single event of copying falls outside of natural laws, but nonetheless the total number of copies, and the survival of some copies under very negative conditions (such as the Maccabean period) appears quite extraordinary.

Everything is an act of God, and everything is natural.

3. Actual physical interventions. The resurrection of Jesus would fall into this category. Many healings can be seen in this or in the second category.

When miracles are divided this way, very few of them fall into the third category—the category that causes most of the trouble. I do not know about all religious traditions, but in my own Christian tradition, even most miracles in the second and third category are intended to communicate rather than to tinker with the natural processes of nature; in fact, one is generally said to miss the point of the miracle if one doesn't understand the spiritual meaning.

So everything is an act of God, and everything is natural.

For example, to believe in the resurrection is to believe that God accomplished certain things for humanity and intended us to understand certain things because of this event. It is not merely a matter of believing that the body of a certain person came back to life. I know of people who believe in the resurrection solely as a spiritual event and yet see the same spiritual meaning as I do. Jesus indicates in John chapter 6 (esp. verse 26) that some people ate miraculously provided food (the physical event), yet did not see the sign (what Jesus intended to teach). It is in the sign that the important content resides, at least in the Christian tradition.

More importantly, I see no difficulty with either of the first two categories of miracles in connection with the arguments I have presented about the hand of God. In fact, one might say that the miracle resides in how one looks at the events and not in the events themselves. The eye of faith lets us see the miracle. And these two categories cover the vast majority of miracle claims.

Most discussions of prayer center on the wrong topics, and test prayer by the wrong standards.

But now let's consider something further that is more troubling for many people. Can we alter God's actions through prayer?

A hurricane was approaching the gulf coast, and thousands of Christians began to pray. "Lord, we need your protection," they said. "Let the hurricane not come ashore where we live. Bless our homes and businesses **and protect them from destruction."**

And indeed, the hurricane moved back out to sea.

Unfortunately, it went ashore further along the coast, where thousands of other Christians, who had also been praying, lost **their** homes and businesses.

This story is a generic one, built of many experiences I have witnessed or heard about, but I believe it demonstrates a problem many Christians have with the efficacy of prayer. I often have trouble getting involved in discussions about prayer, and whether prayer "works" because it seems that these discussions center on the wrong topics, and test prayer by the wrong standards.

Now I want to discuss prayer in relation to the hand of God. Previously I classified most miracles as miracles of communication —situations in which God provides some information, understanding or wisdom. I have suggested that God is most at work when we tend to think he is doing nothing at all; that we classify as evidences of God's activities things that are exceptions to his rules.

God is most at work when we tend to think he is doing nothing at all.

Perhaps there is a sense here in which the words of Jesus to Thomas apply: "Blessed are those who have not seen and yet have believed." We look for the things that are different or unusual in order to discern God's hand moving. We need to look at the mass of things that work in the same way and thus are so consistent that we can base much of our lives on them.

And this leads to prayer. Can people really change the way God behaves? Can people somehow persuade God to change his plan? Can they persuade him to turn aside the course of natural events and respond to the needs, or even the conveniences of finite, mortal human beings?

All of those questions, I believe, start from the wrong point of view. If prayer exists for the purpose of changing God's mind, if it is a way for us to get things or arrange things to our convenience then it's an aberration in God's orderly universe. It also

46

demonstrably does not work. Note that I said **if** it is those things, it doesn't work.

There is a fairly common demand of skeptics that a Christian should pray that a certain mountain be moved, and if it does, in fact, move, then the skeptic will accept the Christian's claims. And if prayer is described as it is commonly described, and if the claims made for it are the ones commonly made for it, then such a demand is quite valid. If I claim that prayer works, and that "working" consists in God providing me with certain things, or taking certain actions when I pray, then it is quite valid to say, "Show me!" After all, Jesus showed Thomas his side, which **had** been pierced, even though he pronounced a blessing on those who believe without seeing.

The time when your faith will move mountains is the time when your faith has you so in tune with God that you want the mountain to move at the same time God does.

But I would suggest that the test is invalid, because the claim is simply wrong. It is not that prayer doesn't work. I am quite certain—through faith—that it **does** work, and works wonderfully. "Do you get everything you pray for?" someone asks. No, absolutely not. But then I don't believe that prayer is the means by which I get stuff. In general, God has provided me with a means to get stuff, and that is the law of sowing and reaping. If you don't sow, you don't reap, and that holds spiritually as well as physically.

So what is prayer?

Prayer is a means of communication with God. Prayer is the way I interact personally in a spiritual way with my creator. What God does with what I tell him and what I ask for is not really up to me. It is not that I don't believe he ever does anything for me. After all,

I'm alive, I continue to breathe, and I have this computer on which to write and format this book. God has done many things for me. How many are miraculous? By my own standards, I have no idea. In fact, many things that I would talk about as miraculous are, in themselves, rather mundane. The reason I talk about them as miraculous is simply the way in which they happened.

I often tell classes on prayer that prayer is more than 90% about getting you onto God's program, and less than 10% about petitions. You commune with God, and God puts you on the right track. The time when your faith will move mountains is the time when your faith has you so tuned with God that you want the mountain to move at the same time God does. I would affirm with scripture that God does perform miracles. (I keep the proviso that we might find that all miracles actually aren't—that they are simply the operation of some of God's natural laws that we didn't know about.) I even affirm with scripture that God acts in answer to prayer. How this works, I don't really know.

Prayer is the means of communication in our relationship with God. If we have communicated, prayer worked.

But getting these things to happen is not the purpose of prayer. In fact, prayer designed largely to get things my way is likely to be very unsuccessful. And in most cases, prayer answered is going to be hard to demonstrate. How do you **know** that your prayer had an impact on a particular situation? The fact is, outside of communion with God, looking through the eye of faith (and faith is itself a perspective) you cannot feel or know that some action is a "special" act of God. Faith sees what the sign is pointing to.

Now this may not seem too exciting. You mean I must pray and pray and pray, and what changes is really me? Isn't there an easier way?

48

Not really. There is no easier way. Our interaction with God is a relationship. That explains why we are to ask, when God already knows. If prayer is about getting the stuff that we want, is there any purpose in asking God, who already knows? But relationships take time. They require communication. There's nothing quite like asking my wife what she thinks, even though I might **think** I already know. Is there any reason to tell her I love her over and over? She already knows. (Anyone who doubts me on this is welcome to try the experiment of silence on their spouse. Just don't complain to me about the results!)

Prayer is the means of communication in our relationship with God. If we have communicated, prayer worked. No, it's not testable, but those of you who have communed with God understand the experience. If we present it as such, and not as a way to get God to bend to our desires, I think we will find our discussions much more fruitful.

If we have communicated, prayer worked.

Creation and God's Power

One area in which God's power comes into question is the issue of creation and evolution. Christians hold very different views on the topic of precisely how God created, while agreeing that ultimately God is the creator. I don't question the spiritual sincerity or relationship with God of people who hold just about any combination of beliefs on this topic. But I will suggest here and in other sections of this book, that the evidence favors evolution. (For an understanding of what I mean by evidence, see the following chapter, *It has been Written*.)

I frequently hear the claim that those who teach theistic evolution take glory from God because he is somehow less involved. But how does God's creative power relate to creation? Are those who suggest that God uses evolutionary processes in creation claiming less power for God? Just as I have suggested in this chapter about other activities, I believe God is constantly and totally involved in everything. He doesn't need to pay less attention to one thing than to another. He doesn't have to create priority lists for the way he acts.

We find in nature a great deal of evidence that God works through processes. Acorns fall. Some fall in good places and germinate and eventually grow into large trees. Many don't make it for various reasons. There is a process of growth and renewal. God is at work in this process of growth. He doesn't choose to miraculously create trees or forests, they grow.

My little Shih Tzu is no less a product of God's action than the first ever creature one might identify as a dog.

We know that there is genetic variation in nature. God didn't choose to make all the breeds of dogs; finite human beings working within God's laws accomplished that. But God was and is there. The human beings exist because of him and so do the various breeds of dog. My little Shih Tzu is no less a product of God's action than the first ever creature one might identify as a dog. He is no less a result of God's action than the smallest microbe or even an atom.

I have a problem with the modern movement called "intelligent design." The problem isn't that I don't believe that the universe is designed. My question is how we are to measure design. My theological conclusion is that God created everything, and that we should be able to discern God in everything. If someone found a way to distinguish levels of "design" in nature, that would be a blow to my understanding of God's tremendous power. That's not because they had proved that God was involved in one place, but because they had shown that God was less than fully involved someplace else.

There is one consideration for Christians about evolution that I think is too often ignored. What do we do about the death and destruction of so many creatures that is involved in the evolutionary process? How can a good God create by a process that leaves a trail of dead bodies?

I'm going to talk about this issue in the following chapters, but here let me simply bring back a concept that I introduced in chapter 2 (Of the Good News)—God treats us with respect. Respect involves granting a little autonomy. I cannot have respect for my children and yet control every moment and every action of their lives. I cannot provide for everything they need and want directly, and yet give them any autonomy, and hence any respect.

We are stewards of God's power.

Creatures have to have the opportunity to succeed, and also the opportunity to fail, otherwise autonomy and choice cannot function. Those of my brothers and sisters who are Calvinists will certainly not agree with me here. I'm suggesting that God gives up part of his sovereignty in order to allow a little bit of sovereignty for each of us. God delegates a little bit of his creative power, so we can have a little bit of creative power to use here. And in order for that delegation, or grant of his power to work and be real, he has to allow things to go wrong.

This is another reason I don't expect direct, miraculous action to solve all of the problems of the world. I believe God expects us, as agents and stewards making use of his power to make things right.

God will not miraculously replant forests that we have destroyed. If we don't do it ourselves, natural processes will take care of it, and those natural processes may take far too long for us to benefit from the result.

Think about it for a moment. We are stewards of God's power. When we wonder where God's power is, the problem may be that we are sitting on it and failing to use it.

The good news is that God's power is available in our lives. It will surely be a shame if we don't put it to work.

God's Gifts and Activity

The separation between "Bible times" and "now" needs to be done away with.

But some are probably asking whether I really believe that God is active now in the same way he was in Bible times. Everything I've said in the last few pages could simply look like some excellent tap-dancing. (I can't tap-dance in real life, but I do it well on paper!) When all is said and done, there are still those stories of God's special intervention in the Bible, and the question remains as to whether these things can and do happen today.

I believe that they do. I believe that anything and everything that God has done in one period of history he can do in another. And subject to the appropriateness of that action to the time, he will do it.

The separation between "Bible times" and "now" needs to be done away with. Certainly there were some unique events, such as the resurrection. Jesus died once and for all, and his particular resurrection was unique in history. But God still can and does act. What I am concerned about is our desire to limit God. Now by "limiting God" I don't mean our common supposition that God can't do great things. I mean rather our supposition that God is **not** doing great things. And part of that assumption is our common belief that when we don't see the fire coming down from heaven, God isn't acting.

But God says that he will act through his body, and that he gives gifts to that body in order to help it to carry out his work. I firmly believe that those gifts continue to operate in the church today, and that it is through those gifts that God most desires to act in the world.

Very frequently Christians are sitting in their churches, maintaining their buildings, polishing up their mission statements and points of doctrinal belief, praying that God will do something to revive the church and transform their community. But God already did his part. He called us, he equipped us, he gave us resources. Why aren't we making use of those resources to transform our communities? Why are there people starving and homeless around our churches? Why do we have missionaries serving, but starved for resources to do their work?

Christians are sitting in their churches, maintaining their buildings, polishing up their mission statements and points of doctrinal belief, praying that God will do something to revive the church and transform their community. But God already did his part.

The power is available. God has sent his Spirit. We're just not willing to do our part of the miracle! Remember what I said previously about the cross. If Jesus had risen from the dead, and the disciples had gone back to fishing instead of proclaiming it, then no transformation has taken place.

There has been a new creation in every Christian. You and I have been made new creatures. God's miraculous power has acted in our lives. My question is this: Where is the proclamation?

Where is God's power? It's right here. God's church has it. We should be very ashamed of our poor stewardship. But God still does transform lives. That is the message of the gospel.

And there is no shame in that!

For Salvation

I think that Christians generally have a very weak view of salvation. I think our view falls far short of what God has in mind. Humanity was originally created in God's image, and that includes both men and women. In the fact that both male and female are included, I think we should find our first hint that it is not the physical form that we are talking about. In fact, I would suggest that the image of God in us consists precisely of that autonomy and creative power that I discussed in the preceding chapter.

We put a low value on freedom of choice, on autonomy, and on creativity. We prefer comfort and safety.

We put a low value on freedom of choice, on autonomy, and on creativity. We prefer comfort and safety. Many, many people will give up their own decisions and their own stewardship in exchange for the feeling that they are safe. But it appears that in the way that God has arranged the universe, physical safety is much lower on the priority list. Spiritual safety is much more assured than is physical safety.

Further, when God made us in his image, he declared what he had made very good. Later, in the Psalms, humankind is called "a little lower than God" (Psalm 8:5). The verse continues by telling us that God crowned human beings with "glory and honor." Again, I'm going to suggest that this position is a little lower than God, a position that includes some of the divine nature, and one of being God's children, comes from our stewardship of God's power. We live and act with much less than the divine intention. One of the clearest teachings in scripture shows how humanity deteriorated after they sinned and left Eden. As a result, we are in serious need of spiritual healing. We are in need of a restoration of the image of God.

The good news brought by Jesus tells us that the image of God can be restored, that spiritual healing is possible.

Now let me provide one note for those whose major concern is with physical healing. I do believe that physical healing comes from God, and is an aspect of the good news. I believe that God does heal miraculously some times. But God heals primarily to show his power and glory and to draw us to him. We may not know very much about the afterlife; heaven and hell seem like such undefined terms to us. People disagree on what's going to happen. We've never seen it, except for some fortunate souls who have seen such things in vision, and then I have to wonder if they really comprehend it. But God *does* know your eternal future, and he knows that the long term is the critical thing—it is what you are going to do together with God.

The good news brought by Jesus tells us that the image of God can be restored, that spiritual healing is possible.

Here on earth you have the task of living within the universe that God has made, of being stewards of what God has given you. You have to live here with the portion of God's power with which he has entrusted you. We think of the parable of the talents that Jesus told (Matthew 25:14-30), and we that it refers to the worldly, physical goods that God has provided us, or some special spiritual gift that God has given us.

But God has given us our lives, our physical powers, and our minds, and those are things of which we are stewards. With our

56

minds and our physical powers we are now capable of destroying the world in which we live. That's a responsibility given us by God when he entrusted us with some of his creative power.

As Jesus said, "The one who is faithful in something minor, is also faithful in much" (Luke 16:10). In the similar statement in Luke 19, the servant who was faithful with a small amount of money was then made ruler over ten cities. I believe this indicates the kind of sovereignty and responsibility that God intends to grant to his people.

But that sovereignty will result from our being faithful in our stewardship of what we have. That includes our lives, our minds, our material possessions, our natural talents, our spiritual gifts, and our time.

Spiritual Healing

Spiritual healing, then, is the restoration of God's intention for human beings. This involves a restoration of our spiritual state here and now, a promise of eternal life, and a promise that those who are faithful in the least will have the opportunity to be faithful in much more.

Spiritual healing, then, is the restoration of God's intention for human beings.

Let me chart some terms to give Christians who are versed in the more traditional terminology an idea of how I'm going to talk about salvation.

Traditional Term	Event
Original Sin	Failure to completely carry out the responsibilities of stewardship
Justification	Orienting ourselves toward God's will and plan, with the intent of accepting the spiritual healing and becoming the person God knows we can be. God offers this freely with the only condition being that we accept.
Sanctification	Walking out spiritual healing, the long process, in which God uses the natural laws of this world, other people, communion with him, and our own errors in making us better stewards of what he has for us.
Glorification	Entering into the new kingdom, in which we become stewards of more as a result of our stewardship here. Notice that it was only the one who was given only one talent (Luke 19:20-27) who has everything taken away. The only way to fail of any reward is never to get involved in the game (the process) at all.
Righteousness	Being in the right relationship to God.
Imputed righteousness	God looks at us as what we can become though his power, not as what we have made of ourselves. We see ourselves and worth very little, God sees us as worth more than we can imagine.
Imparted righteousness	The "rightness" that God gives us through the process of sanctification—an evolutionary process!
Legalism	Thinking that the whole idea is to keep from making God angry by following all

	the rules. (Read the parable of the talents in Luke 19:11-27 again!)
Righteousness by works	Trying to earn the right to do it God's way instead of just going ahead and getting on his program. It's like trying to buy a ticket to a free concert.
Righteousness by faith	Realizing that God made the universe, made the way of salvation, and gave us the power to do something about it, and we're just going to have to work within his (very wide) boundaries.
Holiness	Being a steward of what God has given you.

My theologian friends (and enemies) are not going to like all of these definitions, but I think that the whole concept of salvation has been made much more difficult than God ever intended it to be. If we will look at Genesis 1 & 2 and then at Revelation 21 & 22, we'll see the basic plan. God made it good, and he wants to make it good again. He wants us to go along with him on this, and use our delegated creative power wisely.

You need to find spiritual food and spiritual language that is constructive for you.

That, to me, is salvation. We can describe this process with an abundance of theological terms, but those are all embellishments. They help people with different personalities and different points of view understand what's going on. They are good things, if they help someone come into a closer relationship with God.

Now you can say that my description of salvation is also an embellishment, a teaching that will apply to people with certain backgrounds and personalities. And you would be absolutely right to say that. The language changes, the reality doesn't. My language is just as much a distant, symbolic way of understanding the reality as anyone else's. If you don't find it helpful, go read something else. I mean that sincerely and without hostility. You need to find spiritual food and spiritual language that is constructive for you.

Social Healing

But while you're finding spiritual language that is constructive for you, consider other people as well. I know a number of people who are Calvinists. I used to wonder how their minds worked because I couldn't fathom how they could understand God in a way that seemed so nasty to me.

And yet through contact with them and communication with them I have come to understand that they find a great comfort in knowing that God is in charge. Where I would see a fear of hell and the possibility of God arbitrarily sending me there, they see a calm assurance of God's love and themselves chosen from the foundation of the world. Where I would expect them to quit working because they are predestined to salvation, they respond in action to the love of God. Where I would expect hostility toward non-Christians, because God must have destined them for destruction, they instead love their fellow human beings and go out of their way to care for them.

While you're finding spiritual language that is constructive for you, consider other people as well.

This means to me that even though their vocabulary is different, and their doctrines are different, they are in touch with, and serving

60

the same God as I am.   We are fellow travelers on the same pilgrimage.

I still have problems with many of their doctrines. I will continue to debate them where I see problems with them, but those debates have to do with how we talk about God and how we act in the world, not with the question of whether they are friends or enemies. I also recognize that many of them, and many folks of any number of Christian doctrinal systems believe that their doctrinal system is the only way to go, or at least is absolutely the best way to describe God. I disagree, but that's OK. I may be able to speak more than one spiritual language while they cannot, but I'm still far short of truly understanding the mystery of the incarnation when God crossed the gap from infinite to finite.

Sanctification and Holiness

All of this leads me to these two long theological terms. I use them only so that what I am saying can be connected to some standard Christian vocabulary.

Christians have generally understood sanctification as a process of becoming holy, and I'm going to use that definition here. I want to concentrate on what it means to be holy, or what holiness is. At root, this word has to do with being set apart for God. But there was a broader understanding taught especially in the Pentateuch or Torah. Things that are holy are in God's sphere in a special way. They serve God's purposes and do God's work. People can be specially set aside, as can buildings, places, or things. It was important to be able to discern the boundaries of

Things that are holy are in God's sphere in a special way. They serve God's purposes and do God's work.

things that were holy and things that were not. There was a term for "crossing over" the boundary. The priests were to teach the people to distinguish between the holy and the unholy (Leviticus 10:10).

I believe that all this focus on holy and unholy was intended to make us conscious of what is and is not in God's service, and to bring more and more things into God's service. There are two ways that this can (and I believe should) happen.

First, we can leave off some acts that are not holy and do other actions that are holy. This is the most traditional way of approaching things. We ask what God wants us to do, and do that. We ask what God doesn't want us to do, and we don't do that. I regard this as a sort of first stage Christianity. Some Christians have made this a goal. We will be holy when we quit watching the wrong movies and read our Bibles more. We will be holy when we spend more time in church, and less time at the amusement park.

Is your job construction? Make laying bricks, pouring cement, or building a building frame a holy act.

But then there is a second way—making things that are secular into holy things, extending the reach of God's presence. I would suggest that this is when we start becoming even more like God. When we start to look at everything we do as part of our stewardship of the resources that God has given us, that is when we start to make everything holy. Is your job construction? Make laying bricks, pouring cement, or building a building frame a holy act. How do you do this? Do it to the best of your ability. Make everything you possibly can of what you have and what you do. But also do it in proportion.

If you are a physicist, this applies to your research, if you are a software engineer, to the way you design software, and if you are a customer service representative, to the way you approach your customers.

But for all of these people it also applies to the way they handle the rest of their lives. There is a current television commercial in which a series of people intended to portray undertakers thank the American worker for bringing on early death by overwork. That isn't good stewardship of one's life.

Sometimes people question me about the type of television shows I watch (quite a variety), the books I read, and the types of entertainment I enjoy. They are often surprised by my answers. I watch some shows that include violence, if that is part of the story, and I'm not offended by the portrayal of nudity on screen, again if it's part of the story. (I'm not trying to set standards here, just telling you what I like. I like my movies or television programs to present a unified appearance. A scene portraying nudity, other sexual elements, or violence that is introduced just to excite the audience tends to turn me off to the story.) I enjoy science fiction, fantasy, and mysteries. And no, I don't choose just those written by Christians or with a Christian theme. I have in the past enjoyed role-playing games, and have even written on the subject.

If you are spending all of your time on one thing, even if that one thing is prayer, you may not be getting more and more holy. You may just be getting less and less balanced.

All of these things can be holy. (OK, don't get too upset.) If they are carried out in a good, healthy proportion, and are part of a life dedicated to doing what is right, they are just fine. I would probably do well to add a better balance of physical sports into my life. For me, getting involved in some kind of sports could well be a holy act.

If you are spending all of your time on one thing, even if that one thing is prayer, you may not be getting more and more holy. You may just be getting less and less balanced. Maybe you're spending too much time praying and you need to go spend some time on a water slide. Or perhaps you have read your Bible so long that it's no longer helping God communicate with you. A good light novel might be just what God wants in your life.

Holiness isn't the equivalent of stuffiness. It's not about being obnoxious and straight-laced. It's about a healthy balance. God can be, and is, on both sides of a healthy balance.

We should be ashamed when we portray following God as spending all our time shut away from the world, or as singing only spiritual songs or reading only spiritual books. We should be ashamed when we portray Jesus as a somber person who might be offended by fun, or when we see God as wanting us to spend all of our time on one thing.

It would be a shame, but it definitely would not be the gospel—the good news.

To Everyone Who Believes

Do you have a small concept of "everyone"? Many people seem to. They say, "Everyone knows that!" or "Everyone was at our meeting!" But we all know that not everyone knows, and that far less than everyone was actually at the meeting.

As Christians we often say that God loves everybody. But our concept of everybody can be very, very small. Let's just consider some of the groups we ignore in our everyday thinking about God and salvation:

Our concept of everybody can be very, very small.

- ✓ All of those people who lived before God spoke to Abraham, and after the message was apparently lost following the flood generation.
- ✓ All the cultures other than the Israelites who had no opportunity to hear any message from God before the gospel was proclaimed in the entire world.
- ✓ All of those people who died without ever hearing the gospel message.
- ✓ Those who are driven away from Christ by Christians.
- ✓ Those who honestly can't come to the conclusion that the gospel message is true. (Some may disagree with me that this class of people exists, but I firmly believe that they do.)

If God was sending a message that was for everyone everywhere, why would he send it only to a small group of nomads in the Middle East? Why would he provide such limited distribution?

The answers I've found to these questions will come only partially in this chapter, and partially in the chapter on scripture (It has been Written) that follows. Here I just want to examine God's way of salvation, and what it involves in three areas:

1. Understanding
2. Belief
3. Action

Understanding and Salvation

Christians, especially conservative Christians, commonly assume that one must understand the plan of salvation, and just how it is that God saves us in order to receive it. I question that assumption. I would suggest that it is possible for someone to be saved without even being aware of it.

> **It is possible for someone to be saved without even being aware of it.**

There are three places in scripture that I think suggest this idea.

Before I look at those three passages let me mention the other side of this issue. Not everyone who apparently understands salvation, speaks certain words, and even does deeds in the name of Jesus, is part of God's kingdom. Jesus says:

Not everyone who says to me, "Lord, Lord!" will enter the kingdom of heaven, but rather it's the one who does the will of my father who is in heaven who will enter. For many will say to me on that day, "Lord, didn't we prophesy in your name, and cast out demons in your name, and even perform many miracles in your name?" But then I will testify about them, "I never knew you. Get away from me you who behave lawlessly." – Matthew 7:21-23.

The first of my key passages is the parable of the sheep and the goats (Matthew 25:31-46). I don't think we read this parable very clearly as Christians because our reading glasses have been coated with Pauline theology and we feel that we must somehow fit what it says into the pattern of salvation that we have built largely from Romans and Galatians. (This pattern needs to be modified by reading other books, such as 1 & 2 Corinthians, but that's another topic.)

Jesus commends those who have done right by behaving lovingly and with compassion toward those who are down and out. These people respond, however, with a denial. They don't know that they have been serving Jesus!

They don't know that they have been serving Jesus!

37 Then the ones who pleased the Lord will ask, "When did we give you something to eat or drink? 38 When did we welcome you as a stranger or give you clothes to wear 39 or visit you while you were sick or in jail?"
40 The king will answer, "Whenever you did it for any of my people, no matter how unimportant they seemed, you did it for me."
— Matthew 25:37-40 (CEV)

This is a group of people who do not know they have been doing service to the king, Jesus, but have been doing the service anyhow. I, as a Christian, know that in doing service to others I am obeying a command of Jesus. I probably do not fully understand how that is, but I do have a hint. But these people are unaware of who is receiving the service they are giving.

67

The other side of this comment, which comes a bit later, is that there are those who believe they are serving the king who find out that they haven't been doing so. This suggests to me that what we know, while important, is not the key to our salvation. One form of salvation by works is trying to earn our salvation through correct theology. If we just get everything right, then God will accept us. But Jesus suggests here that we cannot.

This passage fits well with 1 John 4:7-8, which I have quoted before:

Loved ones, Love one another, because love is from God. Everyone who loves has experienced divine birth, and knows God. Anyone who doesn't love doesn't know God, for God is love. – 1 John 4:7-8

Love is not only the prime command of Jesus; it is also the prime indicator of our service to God and our love for him.

Love is not only the prime command of Jesus; it is also the prime indicator of our service to God and our love for him. John continues later in this passage:

If anyone says, "I love God," but hates his brother or sister, he's a liar. For how can one who doesn't love his brother or sister, whom he has seen, love God, whom he has not seen? — 1 John 4:20

This is a passage that we all need to think about any time we're tempted to think that our relationship with God is OK while our relationships with other people are not. God is testing the vertical relationship—our relationship to him—by the horizontal relationship—our relationship to one another here.

That vertical relationship, the one we have with our heavenly father, is the one we're not supposed to judge (Matthew 7:1). It's a command I think is probably the most violated one in all of scripture. But we can look for the fruit—the impact on our relationships with one another (Matthew 7:15-20).

The second piece of scriptural evidence I have for this view comes from Jesus on the cross. When he is asked by the thief, whose only knowledge of him came from seeing him under torture being led to the cross and hung there to die, asked him for salvation, he simply granted it. He didn't have to know the details of atonement, or salvation by faith or by works. He was simply accepted. His knowledge was different than the knowledge of those coming for judgment in Matthew 25:31-46, and he had no opportunity to put his intention into practice, but even the one simple look in the right direction was sufficient for Jesus to accept him.

He didn't have to know the details of atonement, or salvation by faith or by works. He was simply accepted.

Last, there is the more complex expression of this concept in Romans chapter 2. Paul says:

^{6} For he will repay according to each one's deeds: ^{7} to those who by patiently doing good seek for glory and honor and immortality, he will give eternal life; ^{8} while for those who are self-seeking and who obey not the truth but wickedness, there will be wrath and fury. ^{9} There will be anguish and distress for everyone who does evil, the Jew first and also the Greek, ^{10} but glory and honor and peace for everyone who does good, the Jew first and also the Greek. ^{11} For God shows no partiality. – Romans 2:6-11 (NRSV)

69

Now this is Paul, the one who expounded righteousness by faith, and he makes several points, I think rather clearly. It is our desire as Christians to hold an exclusive position that prevents us from seeing this. First, Paul expresses God's impartiality. We should read "Jew" and "Greek" here as encompassing all of humanity. Both stand equally before God. No matter where you come from, if you do good and obey the truth, you will be rewarded. If you are self-seeking and behave wickedly, there will be judgment. This is not righteousness by works. This person is still accepted by faith, by accepting whatever he or she knows.

The Jews did not and do not have an advantage on salvation just by virtue of being Jews. They were chosen, not to sit around and be special people, but rather to be God's messengers in the world. They were chosen for mission.

Being chosen isn't all that wonderful. Isaiah was chosen, and tradition suggests he was sawn in half. Jesus was chosen and he was crucified.

When people in the church talk about replacing the Jews, they don't really understand what they're saying. Being chosen isn't all that wonderful. Isaiah was chosen, and tradition suggests he was sawn in half. Jesus was chosen and he was crucified. Being chosen is a matter of mission, not a matter of privilege. Now if you are on a mission, you will be entrusted with special information necessary to that mission, but you will also have special responsibilities.

Modern Judaism holds that the laws as a whole apply only to the Jews. Those many rules and regulations that many of us look at as a terrible yoke *apply only to the chosen people*. That is the additional responsibility. Those rules were to make them different

70

from everyone else, to make everyone look at them. By seeing them, others were to learn about God.

As Christians we too have been given a mission. We are to be a light to the world. We are to make disciples. But being Christian is a mission, not a privileged state. It gives us responsibilities and puts us on display to the world. That's what being chosen is about.

[12] All who have sinned apart from the law will also perish apart from the law, and all who have sinned under the law will be judged by the law. [13] For it is not the hearers of the law who are righteous in God's sight, but the doers of the law who will be justified. [14] When Gentiles, who do not possess the law, do instinctively what the law requires, these, though not having the law, are a law to themselves. [15] They show that what the law requires is written on their hearts, to which their own conscience also bears witness; and their conflicting thoughts will accuse or perhaps excuse them [16] on the day when, according to my gospel, God, through Jesus Christ, will judge the secret thoughts of all. – Romans 2:12-16 (NRSV).

There are those who accept and worship God, who are saved and will be with God in his kingdom, who do not know even a single word of our Christian theology.

Now notice especially verse 14. Those who don't have the law may do it instinctively, and if you will read the passage again, I think you will see that those who instinctively do the law are recognized for it. This suggests again that there are those who accept and worship God, who are saved and will be with God in his kingdom, who do not know even a single word of our Christian theology.

71

Belief and Salvation

If people can be "saved" without even knowing who Jesus is, much less having a fully developed soteriology (or theology of salvation), what about belief? What does one have to believe? Actually, the word in Greek that we translate "believe" covers a bit wider of a semantic range than does "believe" in English. It refers to faithfulness as well. It means that in "believing on Jesus" we not only believe certain things about Jesus or certain things that Jesus did. We put our trust in Jesus, his message, and his person. We trust God.

As long as we are only seeking our own good, we will always fail to find it.

This is the way that we turn from self-seeking to God-seeking or good-seeking. When we do so, we are on the path to salvation or spiritual healing. As long as we are only seeking our own good, we will always fail to find it.

Somebody out there is going to take what I'm saying here as an excuse not to share their faith and to ignore missions. "After all," they will say, "God can save them without our help." There are two major problems with this attitude.

First, if you see someone struggling with a problem in the best way they know how, but you know a much better way that you could share, wouldn't you share it? Has Jesus done great things in your life? Is your salvation good news? Can you fail to share that?

Second, God has entrusted you with abilities, resources, and powers. Do you want to explain your inaction when you give an account of your use of those resources?
It's not about what God *can* do without you. It's about what God expects you to do with the resources he has given you.

72

Action and Salvation

Some of you are probably hearing "salvation by works" in what I am saying, and it is unlikely I'm going to convince you otherwise. But I believe this is less "salvation by works" than the theology we're teaching commonly on the streets. We teach people that they have to understand certain things and know certain things. That is an intellectual form of salvation by works.

What a person must do to attain salvation is trust God to whatever extent he or she knows and understands.

What a person must do to attain salvation is trust God to whatever extent he or she knows and understands. One must follow the truth where it leads. We can live in rebellion against the right, or we can follow it.

Actual right living is a result of the change in the heart. I will suggest that the change inside is always God's miracle, whether or not we know how, why, or when it happened. When one has the intention to do right coming from inside, and displays its fruit, God is at work in that person's life.

And that's good news—for everyone!

If you belong to Christ, you are Abraham's children, and heirs according to the promise.

— Galatians 3:29

To the Jew First, but also the Greek

Perhaps 4,000 years ago, God spoke to Abraham, called him from his homeland, and told him he was going to become a great nation and be a blessing to all the peoples of the earth (Genesis 12:3). There is no doubt that without Abraham, Israel, and finally Judaism, there would be no Christianity. Yet Christians often assume an arrogant attitude in dealings with Jews, as though we had invented the entire idea.

Yet Christians often assume an arrogant attitude in dealings with Jews, as though we had invented the entire idea.

There can be many arguments about how close Christianity is to its Jewish roots. Some would suggest that we are very different, and that most of the roots of Christianity are pagan. Others would suggest that we are, or we should be essentially Jewish with an added belief in Jesus. It is well beyond the scope of this little volume to argue the details of these differences, so I'm just going to outline my opinion so you can understand the basis for my discussion of the relationship between Christians and Jews, and the broader implications I believe this has for how we need to relate to all people.

Christianity is indeed an outgrowth of Judaism, but of a very early form of Judaism that was quite varied in its beliefs. Protestants have lost a good deal of their own heritage by discarding the apocrypha. Many concepts that became part of Christian theology have their origin during that time period, but it has become largely a mystery to Christians. We know about the final prophets of the Old Testament, and then we know about the gospels and the birth of Jesus, and in between those two things, well, *something* happened.

We Protestants have accepted the canon of Jewish scriptures, while at the same time holding doctrines that certainly appear not to be orthodox by the standard of that list of scriptural books. At this point let me also make a note about terminology. I use the "Old Testament" to refer to the scriptures written in Hebrew that are accepted by Christians, when those scriptures are read and understood in a Christian context. I use "Hebrew scriptures" to refer to those same books when read from a Jewish perspective. The reading can be substantially different.

Borrowing is a standard process in the development of religious ideas.

Amongst the things that the apocrypha introduces are our Christian concepts of good and evil and much of the detail of our concepts of good and evil beings. It also introduced the style of understanding the end time events characteristic of the book of Revelation—that God will intervene to destroy the world as we know it and create a completely new one. It also paved the way for the importation of some of those concepts common in the pagan, especially Greek worlds.

I want to be very clear here that I have absolutely no problem with borrowing or mixing of symbols. I commented once that I really appreciate the symbol of the Christmas tree because it has been borrowed so many times that nobody really knows its original meaning. Israelite religion preceded Judaism. It was different from the Judaism of Jesus' day, and from modern Judaism. But it also borrowed from the concepts of nations around it and developed over time, just as Christianity has done. Borrowing is a standard process in the development of religious ideas.

But Jesus, as a human, came as a Jew of his time, and lived his life as a Jew. Most of his early followers were Jews. As the new religion incorporated people of other backgrounds, it developed concepts that were useful in understanding who Jesus was and how they might relate to God. The more this process went on, the more separated Christianity became from Judaism.

At the same time some of the early texts of Christianity tended to change meaning. The most important of these changes was simply that debates that had once been debates between different Jews, and different factions of Judaism automatically were transformed into debates between two different religions.

Debates that had once been debates between different Jews, and different factions of Judaism automatically were transformed into debates between two different religions.

The things that people of one ethnic group or one religion can say to another become terribly nasty when said about them by members of another group.

This gives us a basic principle. Don't take your cue from the gospels when you start talking about Jews. In fact, the way Jesus talks to other members of his own people is closer to the way we, as Christians, need to talk to one another when it comes to cleaning up our act.

Now please don't take this as an invitation to contentiousness and disunity. But when Christians do things that are clearly contrary to the teaching and example of Jesus, we need to speak up, and we need to do so clearly.

Becoming Spiritual Israel

Being "spiritual Israel" does not suddenly give us special privileges, and doesn't make us superior to the original Israelites. We might think of this more as God adding to the people he is asking to be messengers, rather than replacing one set of messengers with another.

Messengers? Yes! One of our problems with understanding the "chosen people" is that we have an incorrect concept of "chosen." I have already discussed this in the previous chapter. God chose the Jewish people to carry his message, a message that is part of our heritage as Christians. God has chosen us as Christians for a mission—witnessing to his love in front of the world.

Any time you want to criticize the Jews for how they have carried out their mission, you should consider the way we Christians have handled ours.

Any time you want to criticize the Jews for how they have carried out their mission, you should consider the way we Christians have handled ours. Our witness is marred by wars, persecutions, strife, disunity, judgment, and misrepresentation. That is what we need to be concentrating on.

Jesus' command not to judge is a very practical command. When we focus on the faults of others, we tend to get self satisfied. We can't change what others are thinking or doing. But if we kept our eyes on what we do, and the problems that we can fix, that is something we can act on. And Jesus makes it clear that he expects those who are part of his kingdom to take action.

78

Not everyone who says to me, "Lord, Lord!" will enter the kingdom of heaven, but rather it's the one who does the will of my father who is in heaven who will enter. – Matthew 7:21

But there is a further point we need to understand, which I base on what I have just said. God doesn't call us to exclusivity, to be the special ones who have the inside track on salvation. We shouldn't look down on the Jews, from whom we got so much of our own message. But based on the same principle, we shouldn't be looking down on anybody. Are we truly arrogant enough to believe that we have all the truth and the only truth available? Do we truly believe that God has spoken only to us and to the limited set of people in our tradition?

I want to make clear that I am not teaching that every possible set of religious beliefs leads to God. I even think there are dead forms of Christianity that don't lead to God. Just because someone claims the name of Jesus doesn't mean that they are carrying out the mission Jesus gave to the church. I know only the way of salvation **I believe that Jesus is the fundamental fact of salvation.** through Jesus. But I think it is a monstrous accusation to make against God that he would fail to make available as much of his message as is necessary to salvation to the vast majority of people who have ever lived.

The God who died as Jesus Christ on Calvary is, I believe, much more efficient than that. Since I believe that God was especially present in the incarnation, I do believe that Jesus is the fundamental fact of salvation *for everyone*, but as I have said when discussing salvation, it is not knowledge of a particular set of facts, nor belief in a particular set of doctrines, but having a relationship with God that counts.

79

I believe that God cares about all people. To the Jew first and also to the Greek means that God is going to get his message out.

And that's a God it can be a joy to worship!

It Shows that God is Right

Does God care about his reputation? If I read the book of Job correctly, it appears that he does. Satan comes with an accusation before God. Openly, he claims that Job serves God only because he is so blessed. But behind that claim is that either nobody would or nobody could obey God and live a righteous life without that particular blessing.

God's claim is that human beings can choose to be righteous, and in fact that they can be righteous. Job is his prime example for that case. It's interesting to me that Job never finds out about this byplay in the earlier part of the book. He just knows that he is blessed and doing well, and suddenly disaster strikes.

God's claim is that human beings can choose to be righteous, and in fact that they can be righteous.

It's interesting to ask whether God would really use his best servants in that fashion, but I really can't be certain if the conversation between the satan[2] and God is a literary device or if we are intended to understand that Job is a soldier who makes a sacrifice in God's battle.

---

[2] I use "the satan" throughout this chapter, because the concept of Satan as contained in the book of Job is not the developed idea of the devil as taught in Christianity. This "satan" ("adversary" in Hebrew) is a member of God's court whose task in accusation—basically keeping everyone honest.

What is God Like?

If we looked just at this one story, the question of the way God used Job could become the critical question. But since we have the rest of the Bible, we have plenty of other material to work with.

We know that God communicates with us, that he is willing to share our conditions and experience life and death as we know it. We are told that he wants to save as many of us as are willing. But we also know that he lets us make our own choices and take our own actions.

He doesn't say that God's laws are not good. He claims that people cannot accomplish them.

But none of this forms a part of the satan's accusation. He doesn't say that God doesn't care, or that God doesn't communicate. He doesn't say that God's laws are not good. He claims that people cannot accomplish them.

Are God's laws good or not?

⁶ You must observe them diligently, for this will show your wisdom and discernment to the peoples, who, when they hear all these statutes, will say, "Surely this great nation is a wise and discerning people!" ⁷ For what other great nation has a god so near to it as the LORD our God is whenever we call to him? ⁸ And what other great nation has statutes and ordinances as just as this entire law that I am setting before you today?
– Deuteronomy 4:6-7

Israel certainly thought the laws were good. They thought the laws were a gift from God. They thought they were something that could be kept and that good would result from keeping them.

Who is right, God or Satan?

Cosmic Conflict

I think this is the key conflict. God says that he has the best way to live, and the satan says that God is wrong. Unfortunately, by the way we have taught about righteousness, we have tended to side with the satan on this one. We think it is impossible to be righteous.

This ties back into the concept of salvation that I have presented in this book. Salvation is not an affirmation that God's law is impossible to keep and therefore we need the blood of Jesus to take care of the problem. Now I agree that we need the blood of Jesus. The incarnation is the very key to the fact that we have salvation and that we have eternal life. But the blood of Jesus represents both God's power and God's intention. It represents his intention to save (heal and restore) and his power to accomplish that salvation. In fact, this is the power of the creator.

Christianity should be about the victory of good over evil, of God's power in our lives through his Spirit over the power of evil.

We limit grossly God's power by claiming that we have to remain helpless. Christianity should be about the victory of good over evil, of God's power in our lives through his Spirit over the power of evil.

The cosmic conflict, the battle that's going on behind the scenes, is about whether God's power can be part of our lives, whether we can be made clean.

The good news says that God's power is available. The only shame is if we don't make use of it.

From Faith to Faith

One of the tragedies of Christian experience and faith is that it frequently fails to pass from generation to generation. Now many observers of the American scene are likely to think I must be joking. People tend to stay members of their churches, and they are filled with traditional Christian attitudes and values, even when they no longer attend church or make any claims about being Christians.

But those are simply the traditions of Christians. A living, vibrant experience with God seems too hard to pass along, and often children have no idea of how their parents have walked with God, what their problems were, and also their triumphs. In order to share this, we would have to admit that we don't have all the answers—a growing relationship is a seeking relationship.

The problem is that we tend to put most of our work into passing on the traditions of the church, "churchy" behaviors, and sometimes the texts and doctrines of the church.

The problem is that we tend to put most of our work into passing on the traditions of the church, "churchy" behaviors, and sometimes the texts and doctrines of the church. Parents will boast about whether their children are still attending church and whether they are still attending Sunday School. Now there's nothing wrong with passing on good habits. But simply attending church or Sunday School does not mean that someone's faith is still alive.

I would especially mention Bible study—looking at the ancient texts of the church—as a good and valuable activity. But many Christians seem to feel that if they teach their children a few proof texts and get them to know a few of the key beliefs and values of the church and then go to the altar and accept Jesus as their personal savior, they are doing well. They can even throw in a few Bible stories about the power of God—all about 2,000 or more years old.

But ask many Christians where God is in their life, and they're uncertain what to say. Is God currently active? Has God done anything specific to which I can give testimony? Several times recently I have been tremendously encouraged when attending my home church as I have watched a testimony meeting break out in the service as people talk about their personal experiences during just the past week. *That* is passing on the faith, and not just the traditions.

Ask many Christians where God is in their life, and they're uncertain what to say.

A few years ago I asked my mother for some prayer experiences that I could use in teaching. I knew quite a number of stories, because my parents did pass on experiences of their own in living the faith. (The resulting book, Directed Paths, ISBN: 1-893729-22-2, is published by Energion Publications.) When I got her manuscript, I learned new things about her faith walk and how God had led her. That was an encouragement in my own walk, as it has been an encouragement to many of my students as well.

But the principles involved were already expressed in the Bible long ago:

¹ My friends, I beg you
to listen as I teach.
² I will give instruction
and explain the mystery
of what happened long ago.
³ These are things we learned
from our ancestors,
⁴ and we will tell them
to the next generation.
We won't keep secret
the glorious deeds
and the mighty miracles
of the LORD.
⁵ God gave his Law
to Jacob's descendants,
the people of Israel.
And he told our ancestors
to teach their children,
⁶ so that each new generation
would know his Law
and tell it to the next.
⁷ Then they would trust God
and obey his teachings,
without forgetting anything
God had done.
— Psalm 78:1-7 (CEV)

> **"He told our ancestors to teach their children."**

There are several things we need to note in this passage. Each generation needs to pass on the things that God has done, both the things they get from their parents, and also the things that God does in their lives. That generation then passes those stories—not just the data, the *stories*—to the next generation so they will remember what God has done and what God is like.

It is when they understand what has happened in past generations, and see it happening in their own that young people will obey God's teachings. We spend many hours trying to teach our young people the facts of the faith, what has happened, how they can prove it. We teach them the doctrines and the methods of defense. But how much time do we spend simply sharing and getting them to hear their parents' experiences of God in action?

Especially for the young people if it isn't happening *now*, it's not happening. And we get stuck in the past. Perhaps it is because we're embarrassed. Our stories are too small and insignificant, or they are too personal. Perhaps we wonder if someone will think we're crazy. Well, parents, your kids think you're crazy anyhow, why not make it "crazy for God?" Why not tell them about the times that God has led you or when you believe God has answered prayer? You can talk about Moses, Elijah, or Jesus hearing from the God, but are you ashamed to talk about when you have heard?

In this passage, however, I believe Paul is talking about our own faith walk growing as we live by faith. Someone once told me that the way to hear from the Lord more often is to obey the things you have already heard. I agree, and I can testify to that. Faith grows through practice. James said that "faith, if it doesn't have works, is dead by itself" (James 2:17). The inverse of that is that faith is living when it has stuff going on. An active faith is a living faith, and a living faith is a growing faith. That works both in individual lives and in the community.

Faith grows through practice.

There's one more thing we know about living things—they reproduce. **A living faith is a reproducing faith.**

This process requires us to go ahead and experience the gospel—living it, putting it into practice, putting our trust in Jesus, and then being willing to talk about the result. Only then will we both know what has happened in the past and be able to add to that experience. Short of that, we are passing on a dead faith without any action involved.

Christianity is much more like a role-playing game than like a movie or a story book. It's a story that you join and get involved with. It's actually pretty boring if you're not involved. If you have every watched people doing a role-playing game, you will know what I mean. It's not a spectator sport.

Those who have "played" Christianity as spectators will tend to pass on a spectator mentality. Their witness is this: "Come become a Christian and be idle and bored!" No wonder nobody wants to come with them to church!

The good news of the gospel is not just a single event. It is not just a legal transaction. It is not just a set of doctrines that one believes so one can know one is saved. The good news of the gospel is that God is ready to get into your life and change it. He's willing to move forward with you until you reach the goal—holiness, the restoration of the image of God.

I'm not ashamed of that!

¹² For the word of God is alive and active, sharper than any two edged sword, piercing to the division of the soul and spirit, bones and marrow, and judging the desires and thoughts of the heart. ¹³ And there is no creature who is not visible to him, for everything is naked and laid bare to his eyes, to whom we must render an account.

— Hebrews 4:12-13

It has been Written

Sometime in any debate amongst Christians about almost any topic, someone will bring in the Bible. This is quite appropriate. But our understanding of what the Bible says, and how it says it is critical to getting this important part of our relationship with God right.

What the Bible Communicates

When I first returned to the church in 1994, it didn't take very long before people realized that I had training in Biblical languages. Once they realized that, they would stop me in the hallways between services, or in front of the church afterward, and they would ask me questions about the Bible, about things that had been bothering them, or simply questions about faith and whether the Bible was trustworthy.

I soon learned that people didn't want long answers.

My inclination was to provide long answers, going into the details of the background of the passage, and laying out all the options. I soon learned that this was not something people wanted. They generally wanted a short answer about a single point. They wanted something simple and straightforward that they could understand quickly. I don't mean that they were generally stupid people. But they were generally people who weren't going to spend a couple of hours daily in Bible study, nor spend hours over a single text or concept. They wanted to live their lives, they wanted to serve God in those lives and yet they wanted to understand something of God's word.

In order to respond effectively, I had to do a few things. I had to listen carefully to their question. I had to hear overtones of the question, indicating why they were asking that particular question. Someone asking about healing in scripture might be struggling with the illness of a loved one. Someone who asked about the clarity of God's guidance in scripture might be wondering about a major decision in their lives and hoping to find clarity. After hearing these things, I needed to frame my answer in such a way that they could both understand it and make use of it. I had to speak about things that were of value to them, but were also valued by them.

I was answering *my* questions and not *their* questions.

My inclination as a Bible student was to force on them all the things that I felt were important about the text. The person studying Isaiah needed to understand the details of who Isaiah was, the background of the text, the history of its transmission, and all of the translation options. Otherwise how could they accurately understand the original meaning? But if I did that, I was answering *my* questions and not *their* questions.

I could easily decide that they really needed to know what I had to tell them. Perhaps they needed to know it even more than what they actually wanted to know.

There is an important principle of communication here that we need to remember. ***People need to be ready to hear what is communicated, or they won't remember and apply it.***

Let me illustrate this further. I have a passage of scripture that I use repeatedly in teaching and in prayer ministry. I have done so for years. My interest in the passage dates from when I studied it in college. In general nobody paid much attention to this passage until one day someone else came to our church and spoke about it during a time of prayer ministry with our pastor. Suddenly this scripture became important. It was his key scripture. The story of his prayer time and the importance of that passage were passed around the church. The text suddenly became *important*!

Now it's possible that visiting speaker was able to present the text better than I had. It's even possible that people heard him because he was a visiting speaker. More than once I have shared something about the scriptures with another person, only to hear it later from them expressed in a way that reached an audience I was unable to reach. But I think the key in this case was timing. The passage had been spoken at God's time and in circumstances that God arranged, and it met the need.

The passage had been spoken at God's time and in circumstances that God arranged, and it met the need.

Here's another key: ***The communication has to come at the right time and under the right circumstances if it is to have its proper effect.***

It's very easy for those of us with academic backgrounds or academic attitudes to forget that people are not generally influenced very much by a mere collection of facts. They do not go out to get information for information's sake. Rather, they look for facts that they need. Messages about attitudes and relationships can be much more important that messages about facts—and they usually are. I vividly recall being involved in political action during the years of the Reagan presidency. Activists and political scientists would become nearly apoplectic over the factual content of Reagan's speeches. They noticed every factual error, and they noticed a lack of detailed content. But the American people were eating it up. Why? Reagan was presenting an attitude and a vision; the details were less important than the simple fact of how Reagan made people feel.

Activists would try to make people pay attention to their facts, but they were doomed to failure. They needed to address people's needs and hopes and motivate them through their feelings as well, or they were doomed to failure.

We tend to hear what we expect to hear. One further point I believe is very important about any form of communication, and God communicating with humanity is no exception. We tend to hear what we expect to hear. That has an impact on how things need to be said, and it also means that we have to be careful to avoid hearing the things we want to hear when God speaks.

Recently I attended a communion service. During the service, the pastor gave very specific instructions for the different way that they were going to celebrate communion. As people began to rise to go take communion, they all got up and did precisely what they normally did, rather than what the pastor had directed. He had to quickly move communion servers into new positions to accommodate the way people were acting.

I was teaching a Sunday School class that day, so I asked the class about what had happened. Many had not even noticed that the instructions were different or that anything at all had happened. *They heard precisely what they expected to hear, and acted out of habit.* In order to get a message through, the one who communicates must use methods that get the attention of the audience, and must repeat the message in various ways.

So how does this apply to the Bible?

I'm convinced that we have difficulty understanding Biblical inspiration and talking about what it means because we are too much involved with the 21st century fascination with facts. Now I'm not saying that facts are a bad thing or that we ought to be careless with them. We ought to be careful with our facts. But at the same time, very rarely are facts the primary thing that needs to be communicated.

I was asked once in discussion just what it was God was trying to communicate in Genesis, if he was not trying to provide us with a narrative history.[3] I responded that in Genesis 1, God is communicating power and absolute authority, showing what his word can do. In Genesis 2, he is portraying care and personal attention in the creation, his care for each and every creature. In Psalm 104, which also tells about creation, God is talking about his continuing, sustaining care,

I'm convinced that we have difficulty understanding Biblical inspiration and talking about what it means because we are too much involved with the 21st century fascination with facts.

that he is not a creator or made us and then left. The response was, "Why would he take so many words to say only that?"

Those concepts are extremely important, and simply communicating the fact of God's power, his personal attention or

---

[3] For more information on the topic of Genesis and the creation stories, see my internet articles, Psalm 104: God, Creator and Sustainer (http://energion.com/rpp/psalm104.shtml) and Genesis Creation Stories - Form, Structure, and Relationship (http://energion.com/rpp/creation.shtml).

his sustaining care is not sufficient in developing a relationship. I could take the same approach in my marriage. I got married late in life, and I was not used to communicating about how I felt on a regular basis. I could easily have taken the attitude that having once informed my wife that I loved her, it would be sufficient. Why remind her of something she already knows? Why buy a card that says it in different words?

Communication in a relationship is about a great deal more than the data that we pass on to the other person. Communication in a relationship is about a great deal more than the data that we pass on to the other person. It's about who each person is, how they feel, and how they interact. In the same way, the Bible is part of God's communication with us in our relationship with him. We need to find in it the things that help build relationships. Facts are only a small part of that.

Special and General Revelation

You may be wondering whether I believe that God doesn't care about information and accuracy. I believe God does care about those things, and he has provided us with a mechanism to get that type of information—our senses, our minds, and the various methods we have to shift information. This refers to what theologians call "general revelation," the things that we can learn in the universe in general. "Special revelation" is the specific things that God gives to those he speaks to, such as prophets. I'm going to mangle these definitions just a bit as I carry on this discussion, but that will establish our starting point.

There are things we learn by communicating with God that we can't learn by any other means. By direct communication with God I can learn God's will for me. Through scripture and other words that come through special revelation, I can learn about God's plan. But there is no reason for God to provide me with information that is readily available to me elsewhere.

When I go on a trip, I consult a map and perhaps some travel guides. When I want to work on my car, I consult a service manual. When I want to know about God and how he has dealt with people in the past, I consult the Bible and the works of other people who have had experience with God. When I want to know how the world works in a mechanical sense, studying the processes of nature that are sustained by God's power, I use the scientific method.

I do not in any way suggest that my map is useless or incomplete when I go to the service manual for my car. In the same way, I do not suggest that the scriptures are incomplete when I consult a science text. Each of these things provides me with information that is appropriate to its function.

I do not suggest that the scriptures are incomplete when I consult a science text.

But the Bible suggests something else to me. I mentioned Genesis 1, and its message of God's power, and the power and authority of his word. The first chapter of Genesis suggests that not only the scriptures, but the entire world is a product of God's word. In other words, we are studying God's word when we study one another and when we study nature. The kinds of information we can get are different.

Some people will object that nature is subject to interpretation and thus less reliable than the Bible. But the Bible itself is subject to interpretation. It may be interpreted well or poorly, correctly or incorrectly, but we will interpret it. I don't mean by this to suggest that we cannot reliably understand the Bible. There are relatively few things that are in major doubt in the Bible. We tend to focus on the things where people have vastly different opinions, and that gives us the idea that the Bible is hard to interpret.

One thing will make the Bible hard to interpret—trying to make it cover ground it is not supposed to. At one time people thought the Bible was supposed to inform them about the mechanics of the universe. Galileo and Copernicus changed that. At first theologians resisted, but the change was inevitable, because the Bible was clearly not the correct source for the sort of information science was providing.

There is very clear evidence for biological evolution written in the very ground we walk on.

Today we have a similar debate about evolution. Many people will object that the debate over evolution and creation is not at all similar to the debates over the mechanics of the solar system and of the universe. But I will suggest that they are. There is very clear evidence for biological evolution written in the very ground we walk on. People ask me why the Bible doesn't teach evolution. "Why wouldn't God tell us if he used evolution as a means of creation?" they ask. But God *does* tell us that, through his word written in the things he has created. We just want him to provide us with this information in a much easier fashion.

Please don't misunderstand me here. I'm not trying to say that people who disagree with me on evolution are stupid, ignorant, or without integrity. I believe we can disagree on this. But we should eliminate from our vocabulary the accusations, particularly those that would claim that theistic evolutionists ignore what the Bible says. We do not. We understand it differently, and we understand it in a way that we believe is in accordance with God's word—God's word as he writes it everywhere.

Is the Bible God's Word?

I have been known to hold up a Bible in class and state, "This is not God's word." I do this because people are so used to calling the Bible God's word that it seems almost heretical for them to suggest that anything else might be God's word. But I will suggest that all truth comes from God's word, whether the person who "knows" it or "speaks" it believes in God or not. God's word is the equivalent of God's will and God's will sustains all that which exists.

God's word is the equivalent of God's will and God's will sustains all that which exists.

So the answer to the question is both yes and no. The Bible conveys God's word, and in that sense it can be called God's word. But the Bible is not the only source of truth that a Christian can consult. It is not all of God's word. The primary function of God's word is creation. All created things, including you, are in some way God's word.

Inerrancy

My beliefs on inerrancy[4] follow entirely from what I've said above. I prefer this statement: "When you have found God's message for you in scripture, it is always true." Communication has to work within the understanding of the people who are receiving it. You can push the edges, but if you speak totally outside of the cultural and intellectual background, people will simply not hear you.

> **Communication has to work within the understanding of the people who are receiving it.**

Thus the Bible may speak of God acting directly where he may, in fact, act indirectly. Bible writers may convey their message using available information, for example, in the historical books. In Samuel and Kings, the author is clearly drawing on existing chronicles. There is no reason, except for our obsession with the data, for believing that the chronicles from which that author drew were inerrant, nor is there any reason to expect that God would correct errors of chronology. The message of those books, which has to do with how God led Israel and worked with them during the time of the rise of the Israelite monarchy through the exile, is extremely important and also quite clear. That message is a major reason why there are Jews today descended from the Israelites. Other nations vanished from history when conquered by the Assyrians or Babylonians and resettled. But the Jews held on to their identity.

---

[4] See my internet article, Inspiration and Sources of Authority for the Christian, (http://energion.com/rpp/inspired.shtml) and articles linked from it for more information on the doctrine of inerrancy.

The vision of this writer or group of writers helped hold them together. *That* is inspired writing!

God Acts through Communication

And now we'll tie back all the way to our chapter on God's power. I believe that God's primary means of acting in the world is through communication. Some readers may have felt a tension in that chapter between the suggestion that God wants to run his universe through orderly laws and the idea of intervention. The first sounds somewhat like the rules of a game, designed to put all of us on a level playing field. If God then intervenes in the game to perform miracles for some people, but not for all, it seems unfair.

I'm going to suggest that God communicates constantly, and that the primary factor in whether that communication works is whether we are listening. I've already discussed God's communication in nature. Anyone, anywhere can read God's message in the rocks, the message that shows how he has chosen to create. I believe God's Spirit tries to communicate and invites us to participate in his process of communicating and building **Whenever we understand or speak the truth, God's Spirit is active.** relationships. Whenever we understand or speak the truth, God's Spirit is active. Especially when we manage to "speak the truth in love" (Ephesians 4:15), his Spirit is present and active.

This means that everyone has the opportunity to hear from God. Wherever you are, or whatever your circumstances, you can hear from God.

101

So what is the advantage of being a Christian? If you want to be special, then there is nothing. But if you can appreciate the blessing of a body of messages from God, of examples of people who have walked with God, and of guidance for how one can walk with God, then you have a treasure! The Bible is so much more important than it would be if it were simply an encyclopedia of doctrine. It could make us know all the details, but leave us cold, without the relationship.

I believe God chooses to use those methods of communication that build the relationship.

The biggest miracles occur in changing people. And I would suggest here that the biggest miracles occur in changing people. Sometimes that means recreating you from inside into something better than you were. Sometimes that just means guiding you to the place where it is best for you to be. Intervention suggests unfairness, but if God intervenes in the same way for everyone, and our choices make the difference, then God can fairly intervene. There will still remain those miracles through which God reminds us that he is there, and communicates to us who he is. The resurrection of Jesus is one of those. But I keep thinking that sometime God is going to let us know that he really had those all in the plan and fabric of the universe the whole time. I don't know how, but somehow I think that may be the case.

A Clearer Message?

Once in a study group one member asked me a question that has stuck with me ever since. "Why couldn't God just print out his instructions across the sky, so we couldn't doubt what it said, and couldn't doubt that it was miraculous?" he asked.

I think the answer lies in the nature of the universe God has created. We may not like choice very much. We may not like things to be ambiguous and decisions to be difficult, but God doesn't seem to mind. In fact, God seems to like his creatures to have a range of options. He likes us to be able to make choices. Making choices implies suffering consequences. Choice would be rather meaningless of God cleaned up the mess of all our wrong choices miraculously.

That means that when one person chooses to kill, another may well die. Bad things will happen. But that is the price of freedom. At the same time, if God made everything totally clear, and overwhelmed us with his power, we could not exercise that creativity he has entrusted us with. God gives us some of his creative power and he expects us to use it.

The good news is that we can be subject to God, and when we are, we are free to be ourselves.

And that is truly good news!

There was a man in the land of Uz named Job.
That man was perfect and upright.
He feared God and turned away from evil.
In all this Job didn't sin with his lips;
He didn't say anything inappropriate about God.
YHWH spoke to Eliphaz the Temanite:
"I'm angry with you and with your two friends,
because you did not speak correctly about me
as my servant Job did."

— Job 1:1, 22 & 42:7

The Righteous Person

There was once a man in the land of Uz whose name was Job. That man was blameless and upright, one who feared God and turned away from evil. – Job 1:1 (NRSV)

There are some things about the way people read the Bible that puzzle me. One of those is the reading of this text. I have recently read a book by a well-known and respected preacher who claims that God was getting after Job for his self-righteousness in this book. But the fact is that if we read Job without trying to read our preconceived doctrinal ideas into the text, it is a fundamental premise of the whole idea of the book that Job is, in fact, righteous.

It is Job's friends who argue that he must be a failure, that he must be horribly wicked, and that his punishment must certainly be the result of his deficiencies. They simply cannot imagine someone innocent suffering in the way that he does. When the story is finished, even though Job repents in dust and ashes, God gives no indication of what Job may have done wrong. In fact, he indicates that Job had spoken of God appropriately, while his friends have not.

But modern Christian readers tend to read the book from the point of view of Job's friends.

But modern Christian readers tend to read the book from the point of view of Job's friends. We forget that they are the only ones who are unequivocally condemned at the end of the book.

On the one hand, we are totally convinced by our doctrinal positions that people can't be righteous. Some have suggested to me that Job could only be referred to as righteous because of the blood of Jesus. But God presents Job as an example, somebody different from his peers, a testimony to the fact that it was possible to follow God.

On the other hand, we share in the fears of Job's friends. Yes, I believe that fear is the primary driving force behind the words of all of Job's friends. I have had this problem drilled into my head over the five years of my son's illness, leading to his death—his passing on into glory. There were people who constantly wanted to explore reasons with us. Sometimes those conversations were very hard for us.

Fear is the primary driving force behind the words of all of Job's friends. Don't misunderstand me. We wanted James to be healed. We wanted him restored. We prayed constantly and asked God to bring about that result. But we also submitted ourselves to God's will, to accept the course that things took. That wasn't easy either, and I don't even claim complete success today. I still spend some of my prayer time talking to God about what I wanted to happen and how I don't understand what actually did happen.

Some of our conversations were like the ones with Job's friends. To those of our friends who are reading this, if you're wondering if I'm talking about you, it's a good indication that I'm not. There were those who could question what was happening and explore the possibilities without the oppressive feeling of fear, but there were some who could not. I remember vividly one day early in treatment, as Jody and I were entering the children's ward, she said to me, "The real enemy here is fear, not cancer." And I agree.

Job's friends and many people today have operated from the fear that such a thing could happen to them. They want to find a reason, any reason, to believe that they will be exempt.

I believe this is why we are so quick to blame Job. There has to be something wrong with him, no matter what the text says. The most frightful thing to think is that Job suffered all that through no fault of his own.

But that's what the Bible actually says happened. It's a universal principle. You can suffer through no fault of your own.

But I've gone through all of that to get back to the main point: The book of Job makes no sense unless we truly accept the first verse. One reason, other than fear, why so many people can't really get to the message of Job is that they can't accept the first verse. We're all sinful. We've all fallen short. We're all in need of a savior. Nobody is righteous. So Job can't have been.

An entire book of the Bible is built on the premise that one man, Job, was righteous!

Except that an entire book of the Bible is built on the premise that he was!

And with that I think that we Christians should get up out of the dirt, dust ourselves off, ditch the sad looks and solemn attitudes, quit moaning and groaning about what sinners we are, and walk in renewed life. It is possible to be righteous. It's even possible to *know* you're righteous and God won't get mad at you for it.

What you can't do is be God. That's where Job got cut off. He figured he was going to explain to God how to run the universe.

107

That wasn't going to happen. That's why he repented—not because of guilt, but because of ignorance.

[5] "I had heard of you by the hearing of the ear,
but now my eye sees you;
[6] therefore I despise myself,
and repent in dust and ashes." -- Job 42:5-6 (NRSV)

Job admits that his knowledge is incomplete. He even admits that beside God he is nothing. But there is no indication that he was other than a righteous man. He suffered in God's service, but not for anything that he had done.

As Christians we need to be honest about who we are. We are children of God. God loves us. We are redeemed, bought with a price. We are important. We are supposed to love others as we love ourselves, but we need to learn how to love ourselves. When we fail to love ourselves, when we fail to testify to what God has done for us in enabling us to produce righteous fruit, we lie, and we deny the power of God's love. God loves us and values us.

In economics I learned that value is set by what people are willing to pay for something. What does that make you worth?

I'm not ashamed that I was bought for a price!

Live By Faith

What does all of this amount to? What's the bottom line? Are you advocating some kind of easy faith in which all one has to do is love?

I can hardly understand what one means when one suggests that "all" one has to do is love, as though this was simple. I have to wonder if a person who says this has actually tried loving his or her neighbor. Loving and caring for someone else is a difficult thing. It requires motivation. It requires faith. It requires faithfulness.

Loving and caring for someone else is a difficult thing.

Because that's really what a life of faith is all about—keeping steadily to the goal of love, believing that the goal is attainable and worth trying to attain, and faithfully following through on that conviction.

³And not only that, but we also boast in our sufferings, knowing that suffering produces endurance, ⁴ and endurance produces character, and character produces hope, ⁵ and hope does not disappoint us, because God's love has been poured into our hearts through the Holy Spirit that has been given to us. – Romans 5:3-5 (NRSV)

Appendix A: A Fruitful Faith

There are many views in Christianity on the details of salvation and the various terms, events or processes that go into it. I would like to survey some Biblical material which I believe suggests that one always becomes right with God through a relationship mediated by faith, i.e. by the grace of God, but that the faith must always be a faith that bears fruit. No simple set of words, no transaction, no non-productive faith will do. A few of the texts that I will quote go a little farther than that, but I am interested right now in a broad survey rather than the details.

Let me clarify some terminology. The word "salvation" can refer in scripture to redeeming someone from the rule of evil, to a process of spiritual healing and growth, and also to the final entry into the kingdom of God. Looking at texts from this perspective would constitute another essay. I will simply assume it here. Second, I will use the term "Old Testament" for the Hebrew Scriptures for the most part, because I am looking at that body of literature from a primarily Christian point of view.

I will proceed in seven parts:

√   The original pattern from creation through the end of the flood
√   The pattern of the Exodus
√   Messianic prophecy and the new covenant
√   Jesus

√   Paul and fruit
√   General Epistles
√   Revelation and the coming kingdom

(Since each of these is a rather large topic I'm simply going to outline the main points. This is a topic in which I believe one can say that the notion of salvation by a non-producing faith is unscriptural because it goes against the grain of all of scripture.)

1. The pattern

The "sin" pattern starts in Genesis 3 or 4, but can be most clearly seen, I believe, in the contrast between Genesis 1:31 (God saw everything that he had made, and behold it was very good!) and Genesis 6:5, (God saw . . . that the pattern of the intentions of his [man's] heart was only evil continually.) Here we see the simple statement of the state of the world. It is good to recall that we are reading a story here with the moral points made through narrative. If we grant the situation as described in the story, the world is already in serious trouble before God brings on the flood. The focus in this story from the teller's point of view is not the destruction of the rest of the world, but rather the saving of the eight people.

Note here that the problem is not that everyone is running around bothered by guilt. It is also not that they are afraid of death and of hell fire. Rather it is that the entire tendency of their thinking is evil. Thus an atonement that simply removed guilt would not meet the need. An atonement that left their thinking in the same state in which it was before would not be a response to the problem indicated.

This establishes the pattern that I believe is frequently seen in scripture, in particular in narrative form, which follows through all

112

discussions of salvation--grace comes before law and instruction. Let's look at that pattern as it occurs following the flood. Recall that for the eight people described here, they have just survived a harrowing experience--they have experienced a form of salvation from the situation.

God blessed Noah and his sons, and said to them, "Be fruitful and multiply, and fill the earth.
The fear and dread of you shall rest on every animal of the earth, and on every bird of the air, on everything that creeps on the ground, and on all the fish of the sea; into your hand they are delivered. Every moving thing that lives shall be food for you; and just as I gave you the green plants, I give you everything. Only, you shall not eat flesh with its life, that is, its blood. For your own lifeblood I will surely require a reckoning: from every animal I will require it and from human beings, each one for the blood of another, I will require a reckoning for human life.

Whoever sheds the blood of a human,
by a human shall that person's blood be shed;
for in his own image
God made humankind.

And you, be fruitful and multiply, abound on the earth and multiply in it.
— Genesis 9:1-7 (NRSV)

First, there is a blessing which is the result of a rescue, and then there is instruction. We will see the pattern repeated further on in the same chapter.

The same pattern occurs with Abraham who is called out without any particular request of good action recorded on his part, but who simply believes God. But his belief also results in action (Genesis

113

12:1-4; Genesis 15:6). One might even say that, beyond simply accepting that what God said was true, he put it into action--he put his trust in God. God's act of rescue occurs first, followed by God's promise of blessing, followed by the obedience of the person.

2. The Exodus (Especially Exodus 1-20)

In the Exodus, the single greatest narrative type for salvation in the Old Testament, we find the Israelites rescued from bondage in Egypt because they had cried out under their bondage, but without a great deal of cooperation on their part. Moses and Aaron certainly felt put upon by the very people they were trying to rescue. But note that the salvation again comes before the giving of the law--grace before law. But while grace comes before law, law always does come, i.e. there is fruit that demonstrates the reality of the faith.

3. The Messianic Prophecies

Continuing now to two prophecies, one generally acknowledged as Messianic, and the other related to the return from exile with Messianic overtones. Note that the Messianic kingdom, as proclaimed in Old Testament scriptures had both a moral aspect and a political/rulership aspect. We as Christians have separated these into two parts by applying essentially the "moral" scriptures to the first advent and the political scriptures on the renewal of a Davidic regime in Israel to the second advent. When we further reduce the moral side of these prophecies to a legal transaction, and make the first coming of Jesus primarily a process of sacrifice for sin that makes possible acceptance with God, then we move beyond a recognizable connection.

First, the following from Jeremiah:

³¹ The days are surely coming, says the Lord, when I will make a new covenant with the house of Israel and the house of Judah. ³² It will not be like the covenant that I made with their ancestors when I took them by the hand to bring them out of the land of Egypt--a covenant that they broke, though I was their husband, says the Lord. ³³ But this is the covenant that I will make with the house of Israel after those days, says the Lord: I will put my law within them, and I will write it on their hearts; and I will be their God, and they shall be my people. ³⁴ No longer shall they teach one another, or say to each other, "Know the Lord," for they shall all know me, from the least of them to the greatest, says the Lord; for I will forgive their iniquity, and remember their sin no more.
— Jeremiah 31:31-34 (NRSV).

Note that there is no removal of the force of the law in this passage, but rather the possibility of keeping the law, and more specifically the placing of the law in the heart. I would suggest that this prophecy accords with the grace before law pattern in that only the creator can recreate in such a way that the law is written on our hearts, and that it is following such an act of writing that we can talk about living the Christian life or keeping of any sort of law. The actions are clearly the fruit of an act of God in writing them on the heart. In addition, the knowledge of the Lord is again an act of God, that is, it is the fruit. But if we suggest that God can write his law in our hearts, and then we find that it is not, in fact, written there, we would be suggesting that God's word is returning void (Isaiah 55:10, 11).

Again, we have the prophecy of Ezekiel:

²² Therefore say to the house of Israel, Thus says the Lord God: It is not for your sake, O house of Israel, that I am about to act, but for the sake of my holy name, which you have profaned among the nations to which you came. ²³ I will sanctify my great name, which

has been profaned among the nations, and which you have profaned among them; and the nations shall know that I am the Lord, says the Lord God, when through you I display my holiness before their eyes. ^{24} *I will take you from the nations, and gather you from all the countries, and bring you into your own land. 25. I will sprinkle clean water upon you, and you shall be clean from all your uncleannesses, and from all your idols I will cleanse you.* ^{26} *A new heart I will give you, and a new spirit I will put within you; and I will remove from your body the heart of stone and give you a heart of flesh.* ^{27} *I will put my spirit within you, and make you follow my statutes and be careful to observe my ordinances.*
— Ezekiel 36:22-27 (NRSV)

Note here that again, there is no action which earns or brings on the act of God in redemption, this time to redeem Israel from exile, but the act takes place, and includes the cleansing, the recreation and the enabling to keep the statutes. There is again grace before law, but there is law, and there is fruit of the grace given by God. In addition, note that the recreation is part of the preparation for the political restoration. In this prophecy, at least, the two are very closely connected.

While this specific prophecy is made with reference to the return from exile it does have strong Messianic overtones.

4. Jesus

It would appear that Jesus was quite prepared at least to say that he was fulfilling the prophecies of Ezekiel and Jeremiah. In the Sermon on the Mount, he says:

20 For I tell you, unless your righteousness exceeds that of the scribes and Pharisees, you will never enter the kingdom of heaven.
— Matthew 5:20 (NRSV)

Now he has just said that he has not come to abolish the law and the prophets, but rather that he has come to fulfill. Some interpreters suggest that he means not abolish but to fulfill in the sense that he does away with the law by superseding it with something else. But that would be to make "fulfill" mean the same thing as "abolish." And if we allow Jesus to continue to tell us what he really means, we do not find him discussing anything of the sort. Rather, he continues with saying that our righteousness must exceed the righteousness of the scribes and Pharisees. Indeed, he gives a series of examples that point to a greater inward attitude underlying the commands, in fact, a necessity of having the law written in the heart and controlling ones attitudes rather than merely controlling some actions.

Jesus did not here accuse the Pharisees of obeying the law too much as many Christians have suggested, and as the use of the term "Pharisee" in much Christian discourse would indicate. Rather, he was saying that their keeping of the law was not deep enough. (I am not here attempting to paint a picture of the Pharisees as a group, but rather to note what Jesus is criticizing and what he is not. In fact, I would suggest that the criticism Jesus levels is one that might well be made by one Pharisee against another.) It is a rather tough ethic that Jesus teaches in chapter five of Matthew, including the command to love your enemies and finally to "be perfect as your heavenly Father is perfect." Tough stuff! The Old Testament has nothing on this as demanding moral teaching. In fact, much of it can be traced to the Old Testament.

Now for Jesus' approach to salvation. He says in Matthew 7:21: "Not everyone who says to me 'Lord, Lord,' will enter the kingdom of heaven, but only the one who does the will of my Father in heaven." He continues to list people who have exercised miraculous powers in his name and yet if they have not done his

Father's will, they will not enter the kingdom! I could easily see someone arguing *pure* righteousness by works from this passage, but Jesus was not afraid to put it in precisely those terms. In fact I believe that he was talking about living out the enabling provided by grace and received through faith which was already the redemption pattern throughout the Old Testament.

Jesus goes even further in Matthew 25:31-46, where he separates those entering the kingdom based on what they have done for the "least of these who are members of my family" (NRSV). The measurement is the fruit. Those who have received the grace through faith will produce the fruit. But Jesus is quite willing to talk about it purely from the point of view of the fruit, because the fruit is also an indication of what has happened in the heart already.

Let me note here briefly that Jesus also espouses the two laws, love to God and love to neighbor, which we will see in the general epistles. These are key texts about the content of righteousness. It is possible also to look for the wrong variety of fruit. In every case where fruit is required it is of the appropriate attitude and behavior variety. It is not of the correct understanding of doctrine, or of history, or of some other detail. Doctrine is to be judged as well by its fruit (but that's another topic).

5. Paul

I will only quote one passage from Paul, though I will note that Paul regularly gets into discussion of the proper behavior, and does so generally after he has discussed the nature of the salvation provided by grace. I will take my example from Galatians, known as Paul's strongest statement of salvation, though some might suggest Romans was even stronger. (I wouldn't bother to argue with either!)

118

16 Live by the Spirit, I say, and do not gratify the desires of the flesh. 17 For what the flesh desires is opposed to the Spirit, and what the Spirit desires is opposed to the flesh; for these are opposed to each other, to prevent you from doing what you want. 18 But if you are led by the Spirit, you are not subject to the law. 19 Now the works of the flesh are obvious: fornication, impurity, licentiousness, 20 idolatry, sorcery, enmities, strife, jealousy, anger, quarrels, dissensions, factions, 21 envy, drunkenness, carousing, and things like these. I am warning you, as I warned you before: those who do such things will not inherit the kingdom of God. 22 By contrast, the fruit of the Spirit is love, joy, peace, patience, kindness, generosity, faithfulness, 23 gentleness, and self-control. There is no law against such things. 24 And those who belong to Christ Jesus have crucified the flesh with its passions and desires. 25 If we live by the Spirit, let us also be guided by the Spirit.
—Galatians 5:16-25 (NRSV, emphasis mine).

Here Paul, who has proclaimed grace received by faith, nonetheless says that those who practice the evil things he lists will not inherit the kingdom of God. I would suggest again, that while Paul would strongly state that salvation is always by faith, he would expect that faith to be one that produced fruit, just as all of the other Biblical writers or sources we have quoted thus far. He continues by contrasting the fleshly life with what the life of the spirit actually is.

6. General Epistles

The topic of salvation in the book of Hebrews is rather involved. For now, let me simply note that the basic message of Hebrews is endurance to the end so one can receive the prize. The idea that there must be fruit is apparent throughout the book. Note especially chapter 6:1-8.

James compares a faith that has no fruit to the faith of demons, which is certainly not a saving faith (James 2:19). But one of the best descriptions of faith and its fruit is in 1 John. "If we say that we have fellowship with him while we are walking in darkness, we lie and do not do what is true; but if we walk in the light as he himself is in the light, we have fellowship with one another, and the blood of Jesus his Son cleanses us from all sin" (1 John 1:6, 7 NRSV). One may suggest that "fellowship" and "salvation" are two different things, but the last clause suggests otherwise.

The content of such fruit is opened up in 1 John 3:18 "Little children, let us love, not in word or speech, but in truth and action." And further, "Beloved, let us love one another, because love is from God; everyone who loves is born of God and knows God. Whoever does not love does not know God, for God is love" (1 John 4:7-8 NRSV). Now note again that this suggests that this is related directly to salvation, because we are told that one who does not love does not know God. This reminds me, on the flip side of the coin, of Jesus' statement in Matthew 7:23, "I never knew you."

And for those who would suggest that they can love God without loving one another, we have 1 John 4:20: "Those who say, 'I love God,' and hate their brothers or sisters,' are liars; for those who do not love a brother or sister, whom they have seen, cannot love God whom they have not seen." Often we are told that the command to love God is more important than the one to love our neighbor, but here we are told that our love for God must be demonstrated in love for our neighbors. This is the bottom line fruit.

7. Revelation

Finally, we see that fruit is involved in the final entry into the kingdom. Those who are inside the New Jerusalem are those who have washed their robes (Revelation 22:14), while "outside are

120

dogs and sorcerers and fornicators and murderers and idolaters, and everyone who loves and practices falsehood" (Revelation 22:15 NRSV). One can see the great fight against evil throughout the book, but those two texts kind of summarize the approach.

Conclusion

I would suggest from all of this that there is one pattern for relationship with God expressed in scripture in many different ways and at different times. God calls, God offers grace, it is received by faith, and it produces fruit. The fruit it produces is specifically love for one's neighbor and even one's enemies, by which one demonstrates love for God.

Index

Scripture Index

Add excitement to your study of God's word with these books from
Energion Publications:

	Who's Afraid of the Old Testament God? by Alden Thompson. Discover the God of grace reflected in Old Testament Passages. Price: $13.99.
	What's in a Version? by Henry Neufeld. Are you confused by the number of Bible versions in English today? Get some help in choosing the best Bible version for you. Price: $12.99.
	Daily Devotions of Ordinary People – Extraordinary God by Jody Neufeld. Start your spiritual day with a challenging daily devotional. Price: $19.99
	52 Weeks of Ordinary People – Extraordinary God by Jody Neufeld. Selected devotionals for small prayer and study groups, priced to let you buy copies for the whole group. Price: $7.99.
	Directed Paths by Myrtle Blabey Neufeld. Inspiring stories of God's guidance in the life of a missionary. Price: $7.99.
	To the Hebrews: A Participatory Study Guide by Henry Neufeld. Study this important book of the Bible in-depth with study questions, suggestions, and notes. Price: $9.99.
	Revelation: A Participatory Study Guide by Henry Neufeld. Take a new look at the book of Revelation and find spiritual value even when you disagree on last day events. Price: $9.99

Order direct at http://www.energionpubs.com (Phone: 850-968-1001) or buy from one of the fine internet retailers who carry our books. Ask about quantity and non-profit discounts. Dealer inquiries welcome.

www.ingramcontent.com/pod-product-compliance
Lightning Source LLC
LaVergne TN
LVHW011204080426
835508LV00007B/597